THE LAWYERS LAW OF ATTRACTION

MARKETING OUTSIDE THE BOX BUT INSIDE THE LAW

Hillel L. Presser, Esq., MBA

BROOKLINE PRESS, LLC

Info@BrooklinePress.com | www.BrooklinePress.com

The Lawyers Law of Attraction

By Hillel L. Presser, Esq, MBA

Copyright ©2012 by Brookline Press, LLC.

Published by Brookline Press, LLC

800 Fairway Drive, Suite 340

Deerfield Beach, Florida 33441

Tel: 561-953-1322

www.brooklinepress.com

e-mail: info@brooklinepress.com

ISBN 978-0-9886710-0-3

AUTHOR BIOGRAPHY

Hillel L. Presser, Esq., MBA is an esteemed and successful Asset Protection Attorney, Marketer, Author, Speaker, and Entrepreneur.

Hillel Presser operates a very successful nationwide Asset Protection law practice in Deerfield Beach, Florida. The Presser Law Firm, P.A. represents individuals and businesses in connection with the establishment of comprehensive asset protection plans that incorporate both domestic and international components.

Hillel Presser has been featured in numerous newspapers and magazines, among them Forbes, Sports Illustrated, the Robb Report, the Houston Chronicle, and the Los Angeles Times. He has also appeared on several radio and television networks such as FOX, BRAVO, NBC, ABC, and CBS and has been profiled in the international press in Canada, Germany, Greece, Ireland, and the United Kingdom. He has represented some of today's most well-known business owners, celebrities and professional athletes.

Hillel Presser has authored several books and articles on Asset Protection and Marketing including Financial Self – Defense, The Lawyers Law of Attraction, Asset Protection Secrets, Financial Self – Defense (Revised Edition), Asset Protection in Financially Unsafe Times (foreword), and Captive Insurance Companies (foreword) just to name a few.

Hillel Presser graduated from the School of Management at Syracuse University where he was one of the first students to major in entrepreneurship. He then obtained his law degree from Nova Southeastern University where he was awarded the "Book Award" for the highest academic achievement in business entities and corporations. He has also completed his masters in marketing at Lynn University.

Hillel Presser sits on the President's Advisory Council and Ambassador Board for Nova Southeastern University and currently participates as an active board member for several non-profit organizations for some of his professional athlete clients. Mr. Presser also served as an Adjunct Faculty Member (Law) at Lynn University.

Hillel Presser grew up in Rochester, New York and now resides in Palm Beach County, Florida.

LAWYER MARKETING, LLC

Lawyer Marketing, LLC is a lawyer marketing company focused solely on the needs of lawyers who are looking to better market their practices. The company has the unique distinction of being created by a successful, practicing lawyer for lawyers. With both online and offline resources available, the company can serve as an aid to any lawyer seeking to increase either the quantity or quality of your clients.

Contact us today to schedule a complimentary preliminary marketing consultation to assess your specific marketing needs:

www.LawyerMarketingLLC.com

Info@LawyerMarketingLLC.com

800 Fairway Drive, Suite 340

Deerfield Beach, Florida 33441

(954) 354-1990

ACKNOWLEDGMENTS

This book is dedicated to the loving memory of my grandparents, Florence and Sidney. I'd also like to extend deep gratitude to my parents, Stephen and Suzanne, as well as my sister, Shifra and grandmother, Marcia for all the love and support they've shown me throughout the years. Although I've come a long way since I left upstate New York, I felt that you were all with me throughout my journey.

Thanks to my wife Ashley for her unconditional love and support. Words can't express how much I appreciate you. You're truly my best friend.

Last, but not least; thanks to all my clients who have helped me as much as I have helped them.

TABLE OF CONTENTS

Introduction

What do the late Johnny Cochran and Gloria Allred have in common? The answer may be more than you think. Aside from the fact that they both have superstar attorney written all over them, both were masters at marketing. You may be thinking to yourself that you don't remember any particular advertisements or merchandise that bears either of their names but you do know their names. You can probably conjure either of their faces without hesitation and you may even be able to think of an instance where you saw them on television and found yourself particularly captivated (or revolted) by something that one of them were saying. No matter how you feel about them as lawyers or even as people, the point is that you feel something about them. You're not just aware of who they are but you feel as if you have a sense of their personal politics and quirks. That's not just marketing, it's smart marketing. It's the kind of marketing that companies pay huge amounts of money for. It's the kind of marketing that you need to be implementing now, right now!

This isn't the only marketing book ever written. But it is the only marketing book written especially for lawyers by a successful lawyer. This book isn't a substitute for a marketing department. But it will provide you with solid advice that will help you advance your marketing skills. This book will teach you things that you didn't learn in law school, things that you can't learn by working with or for another attorney. In this book what you'll find are tips, tricks and techniques that will make your efforts to market yourself and your law practice more successful. This isn't simply a marketing book. This is a marketing book, which focuses exclusively on lawyer marketing.

You may be thinking that there are more important things for you to be considering. After all, you're a lawyer and by definition your job is an important one. You're a superhero of sorts, someone meant to uphold the law. But ask yourself a question: how well can you do your job if no one knows what it is that you actually do? Imagine for a moment that there is someone somewhere who has come up with a new type of car, one that is able to both drive underwater and on land. You may think that something like this would not only be news, but news that went viral and fairly quickly. And you'd only be partially right. The invention of such a car would be newsworthy but it would only be news if the inventor came forward with the invention and made an effort to let as many outlets as possible know about its existence. If no one other than the inventor knew about the car it wouldn't be any less of an achievement. Similarly legal marketing isn't meant as a replacement for brilliantly arguing a case. It's meant as a means to bringing you more cases by giving people a sense of just how confident you are in your skills.

Law has always been my passion. But it hasn't always been my job. Before finishing law school and passing the bar I had more businesses than I can count. And in every single instance I worked to market those businesses. There were some huge successes but there were also some spectacular failures. If you show me someone who claims to never have failed I'll turn that person around and show you either a liar or someone who's never truly tasted success. Henry Ford, one of the biggest success stories in the auto industry, was once quoted as saying that "failure is the opportunity to begin again more successfully" and that's as true for marketing as it is for anything else.

I knew that passing the bar and becoming a lawyer was only one piece of the puzzle. In order to become and remain successful I knew I needed to differentiate myself from all of the other lawyers working.[1] I also knew that I couldn't do it alone and that there was no shame in asking for help when I needed it. Consider this book the answer to many of the marketing questions you may not even know you had. And consider me your mentor, navigating you through the often tricky terrain of legal marketing. There are some tips that will work okay, others that'll work better than expected and some that'll make you smack your head and exclaim, "Why didn't I think of that?!" Feel free to mix a little of this and some of that until you come up with a marketing plan that works for your practice and compliments your personality.

Who is this book for?

This book is for any lawyer who wants to increase both the quantity and quality of their clients. It doesn't matter if you're a solo practitioner, working for one of the largest firms in your area or somewhere in between.

Who is Hillel Presser and why should you trust him?

I am an esteemed and successful Asset Protection Attorney, Marketer, Author, Speaker and Entrepreneur. I've created a multimillion-dollar law firm and continue to practice, I'm not some guy who decided to get into marketing because I couldn't cut it in the law field.

---

1   As of September 1, 2011 there were approximately 91,368 lawyers who were licensed to practice law in the state of Florida according to www.floridabar.org.

What's this book about?

Chapter 1: Marketing Basics

This chapter focuses on what you should focus on before doing anything else in terms of your marketing. Specific information is provided on both time management and budgeting.

Chapter 2: Knowing Your Market

In this chapter you'll find information on how to research your clients and your competition. There'll also be insight on how and why you should learn from those who came before you. This chapter is separated into two parts. The first part focuses on identifying your market. The second part focuses on reviewing previous marketing campaigns as they relate to your core clients and working on ways to learn from them.

Chapter 3: Carving a Niche

This chapter will explain the importance of who you are and what you're selling. This chapter includes a formula which will help you to find your own niche and provides insight into the importance of mastering a specialty.

Chapter 4: Branding

This chapter is all about creating a brand identity. This chapter is separated into five parts. The first part focuses on defining what your brand is. The second part focuses on differentiating your brand from that of your competition. The third part focuses on ways to harness creativity. The fourth part focuses on ways to harness uniqueness. The fifth part focuses on creating an overall brand identity.

Chapter 5: Becoming an Expert

This chapter will show you how to build and boost your credibility. It will also teach you how that credibility is maintained. Specifically this chapter will help you to hone in on what your specific expertise is and the ways in which you can share it. Additionally this chapter will show you the difference between selling your services and sharing your services.

Chapter 6: Networking

This chapter is all about relationships and referrals. It's separated into two parts. The first part is all about how to best connect to both social and professional peers and ways in which to build your network. Sites such as Linkedin and Meetup are highlighted as a part of this process. The second part focuses on how to obtain referrals.

Chapter 7: Making Media Work - Social Media

This chapter covers popular social networking sites such as Facebook and popular social sharing sites such as YouTube and provides information on how to seamlessly incorporate them into your legal marketing strategy. This chapter focuses on both social networking and social sharing sites; providing information on sites which are available so that you can decide which ones will work best for your practice.

Chapter 8: Making Media Work - Online Marketing

In this chapter you'll find information on personal websites, blogs, SEO, pay-per-click ads and other ways to get information about your practice to the people who could utilize your services. This chapter is separated into four parts. The first part focuses on websites. The second part focuses on blogs. The third part focuses on newsletters. The fourth part focuses on pay-per-click ads.

Chapter 9: Making Media Work - Public Relations

In this chapter you'll find information about press releases as well as how to secure television, magazine and radio placements. This chapter is separated into two parts. The first part focuses on the type of legwork that you'll need to do. The second part focuses on finding the type of outlets that are best suited for your practice.

Chapter 10: Traditional Marketing

This chapter will showcase information on traditional marketing opportunities such as sponsorships, direct mailers and tradeshows.

Chapter 11: Becoming a V.I.P.

This chapter will focus on the importance of following bar rules while marketing your practice as well as the importance of values such as integrity and persistence.

Resources/Index

This section will provide information on the websites mentioned throughout the book as well as serve as a vendors list. For ease of readability, this area is separated by chapter so that all of the similar vendors and services are listed together.

How do I know I need this?

To answer this question, you'll need to ask yourself two things: Do you want more clients and do you want clients who are better suited to your skills? If you answered "yes" to one or both of those questions then you need this book.

When is the best time to get started?

Now. Right now. Turn the page and we can begin.

Make the decision to make lawyer marketing a priority!

If at any point in this book you find that you have questions, need clarification or are looking for a more personalized approach I invite you to reach out to me for a one-on-one consultation. I can work with both private practice and large firms and look forward to helping you address your marketing needs.

Contact us today to schedule a complimentary preliminary marketing consultation to assess your specific marketing needs:

www.LawyerMarketingLLC.com

Info@LawyerMarketingLLC.com

800 Fairway Drive, Suite 340

Deerfield Beach, Florida 33441

(954) 354-1990

Chapter 1: Marketing Basics

When it comes to marketing your legal practice there are so many aspects that you have to take into account. And somewhere between worrying about whether you're doing everything you can to get the most from your market or whether your online efforts are working, you may realize that there were certain critical factors that you didn't consider. This doesn't have to be an inevitability. It's been said that those who fail to plan are essentially planning to fail, and that's not a club you want to be a member of. Remember that the only guarantee in marketing is that there are no guarantees in marketing. So you need to be armed with the basics, ready to put in the necessary work hard.

This chapter is separated into two parts.

The first part focuses on time management.

By the end of part one you'll be able to do all of the following:

* Identify how much time you truly have to devote to your lawyer marketing efforts.

* Identify what aspects of your marketing you should be prioritizing.

The second part focuses on budgeting.

By the end of part two you'll be able to do all of the following:

* Formulate a basic budget for your marketing.

What you'll need for this chapter:

* Your schedule for the next 3-6 months.[2]

* One of your current business cards.

* A pencil and a piece of paper or an empty computer file.

* An internet connection.

Time management

Even the most basic marketing strategies are going to require that you take the time in order to implement them properly. While the hours you put in doesn't need to be consecutive it does need to be continuous.

<u>How much time do you really have?</u>

There are 24 hours in a day and it's not humanly possible for you to spend every one of them working. And developing a marketing plan for your practice counts as work. It's important that you take the time to honestly assess how much time you have to commit to this endeavor without compromising the amount of time that you have to put into other projects. Ask yourself the following questions:

1) How many hours a week are currently devoted to your practice? This should include not only the hours you spend in the office but also the amount of time you spend traveling to and from work or to clients, any work you do at home and any other activities you do related to your practice, like teaching classes or answering questions on a legal help line.

---

2   This schedule should include any important dates that you need to be aware of and in that vein should include both personal and professional information.

2) What's your social life like? Do you go out to dinner on a regular basis or attend a lot of charity events or are you generally home and in bed by 9pm?

3) Are you a procrastinator? Do you put projects off until the last possible minute?

There are no right or wrong answers to these questions but it's highly important that you answer them honestly. The end goal is to determine how much extra time you really have as opposed to how much extra time you think you have. Marketing efforts can be undertaken even if you only have 30 minutes to an hour every day to devote to them, you just have to be realistic about the potential outcomes.

You know now:

* That you need to be honest about how much time you realistically have to devote to your marketing efforts.

You're now considering:

* How much time you really have each week to devote to marketing efforts.

Try this: https://www.toggl.com/. Toggl is a website that helps you track the time you spend doing each project. It can be a good way to help determine what percentage of your time certain aspects of your practice are currently taking. Additionally, it can also be used across a variety of platforms making it easy to implement and use. Both free and paid plans are available.

<u>What should you be spending your time on?</u>

When you begin to think about marketing it can be very easy to become overwhelmed. However, what you need to be focused on in terms of your marketing in the very beginning are the absolute essentials.

What the essentials are will vary based on the type of practice you have. For example, in a highly competitive market it may be imperative that you immediately invest in ad space in a prominent location. But if you're a low-key environmental practice it may be more necessary for you to focus your marketing energy on finding green ways to promote your services. The single commonality that exists for all practices is that you're going to have to expend some energy doing research. More in depth information on this can be found in the "Knowing Your Market" chapter.

You know now:

* That what's essential for one lawyer in terms of marketing may not be essential for your practice.

You're now considering:

* What your market may be.

Exercise: Write out the 3-5 key traits of your practice. Are those traits related to the services you offer? Are they related to the type of law you practice? Are they a mix of both things? Which if any of those traits can be integrated into your marketing? Honestly assess whether or not they make sense to incorporate into your marketing now or if they should be included in future marketing.

Budgeting

Whether your budget for marketing is $100 or $100,000 you want to make sure that your money is going towards efforts that make sense for your practice.

Formulating a basic budget for your practice

Before you start to think about what you're going to spend money on you have to know how much money you have. Let me rephrase that: you have to know exactly how much money you have, down to the last cent. And when you start making purchases you need to know exactly how much money you are spending. While it's okay to round up to the nearest dollar when guessing what you think things may cost, it's important that when you know the exact price that's the number you're working with.

How much you have to spend and what you'll ultimately spend it on will depend on you but here are some key thoughts to keep in mind:

* How much money is honestly available?

You need to seriously consider this. How much money is available for your marketing efforts? Do you have a separate account set aside or are you funding this out of pocket? Do you need to consult with anyone else before you spend any money? Answering all of these questions will help you to determine how much money can be spent on your marketing efforts. This isn't an amount you want to estimate so take the time to answer the questions fully.

* Be able to tell the difference between marketing materials you need and marketing materials you want.

Business cards are essential. Stainless steel business cards embossed with the name of your practice aren't essential. It's important before you spend a single dime that you think about what it is you absolutely need to have. And then look over that list and make sure that you genuinely do need those items as opposed to wanting them.

* Identify what's worth a higher price tag and what isn't.

There are going to be items that you can get at a discount and items that are worth you splurging your money on. Now's the time for you to make note of what those items are. There's no shame in clipping coupons or checking out sales for things like brochures from companies you know you can trust. And social media marketing can be free in a lot of cases. But there are things that are worth the higher price tag in the short term because they'll help ensure that your marketing is as polished as possible. Therefore take some time to think about what's especially important to your lawyer marketing efforts. If you're looking to create a lot of advertisements then invest the money in a great photographer and/or graphic designer. If you want to make an unforgettable first impression think about investing in memorable business cards. By figuring out what's most important to you, you can better gauge where it's best for you to spend your money.

You know now:

* That what's important isn't how much money you have for marketing but what you're doing with it.

* There is no one size fits all budget for lawyer marketing.

* That you need to be aware of exactly what you're spending.

* That you need to be aware of exactly how much you have to spend.

* That what you need and what you want will not always be the same thing.

* That there are some items that are worth paying more for.

You're now considering:

* What items should be prioritized in your budget.

Try this: Go to

http://office.microsoft.com/en-us/templates/marketing-budget-plan-TC001145556.aspx and you'll find a free template to help you with your marketing budget. While you need a Gmail account to access and edit it, the account is free and when customizing the template you can add in what you're spending money on as opposed to being limited by what the sample spreadsheet has to offer.

Next: Knowing Your Market

Chapter 2: Knowing Your Market

Do you know who you're marketing to? Do you know who your competitors are marketing to? Are you attempting to re-invent the wheel? The answers to those questions are probably "no," "no," and "yes." That needs to change. Now. Ignorance of the law doesn't negate the need to follow it. Ignorance of your market doesn't negate its existence or its needs.

This chapter is separated into two parts.

Part one focuses on identifying your market including the audience you should be targeting as clients and your true competition.

By the end of part one you'll be able to do all of the following:

* Identify your market in specific terms.

* Identify who you should be marketing to.

* Identify how you should be marketing.

* Identify your specific competition.

Part two focuses on looking at past marketing successes and failures as they pertain to your core clients and working on ways to learn from them.

By the end of part two you'll be able to do all of the following:

* Identify past failures with your market.

* Identify past successes in your market.

* Identify opportunities to turn failures into success.

* Identify the difference between success and stagnation.

What you'll need for this chapter:

* One of your current business cards.

* Any additional marketing material you may have.[3]

* A pencil and a piece of paper or an empty computer file.

Knowing your market pt. 1: Identifying your market

Who are you currently marketing to?

First, answer this question: Who are you marketing to?

Are you happy with your answer?

Feel free to rethink it, but don't over think it.

Who are you marketing to?

Is your answer broad? If so, it may be too broad.

If your answer is similar to "People who need legal services" or "People who need my legal services" then you're answer is only partially right. And in terms of legal marketing, being partially right about who your clients and potential clients are is as bad as being wrong. In this instance it's because of the fact that you're failing to include a portion of your market, then you're missing the opportunity to present your services to them.

Is your answer specific? If so, it may be too specific.

If your answer is similar to "Men in their late 30s+ who own their own companies and have a current net worth of over $5 million" or "Women seeking annulments as a means to dissolve a marriage of more

---

3 If you don't have additional marketing material it's okay.

than a year." then your answer is still only partially right. And in terms of legal marketing, being partially right about who your clients and potential clients are is as bad as being wrong. In this instance, it's because of the fact that you're putting too many restrictions on who your potential clients can be. While it's good to specialize, you need to be sure that you aren't specializing to the point that you create a potential client pool that can't be or won't be replenished.[4]

You know now:

    * Who you've been marketing to.

You're now considering:

    * Whether or not this portion of the market is the segment you should have been focusing on.

Exercise: Using your business card or mailer, look at it critically. Can you tell who it's supposed to be appealing to? Do you think it would be appealing to the clients you were trying to market to?

<u>Who should you be marketing to?</u>

Consider this, in order to understand your potential market you need to know who you are and exactly what services you're capable of and willing to provide. Identifying potential clients begins by looking at the person in the mirror.

Answer the following questions: divorced or separated parents of varying income levels[5] who seek a quick resolution to their dispute.

---

4   More on specialization will be covered in the next chapter.

5   These income levels should still be within your fee schedule.

Knowing exactly who you should be focusing your legal marketing efforts towards makes it easier to research your market.

Market research, while important does not need to be overwhelming. You don't need to spend countless hours online looking up information, or days asking people to fill out surveys and questionnaires. You do, however, need to be aware of your surroundings and willing, if necessary, to change any pre-conceived notions regarding who your market is supposed to be.

Answer the following questions:

1) Is there a need for the type of law you practice where you're currently located or do you have the money and time to travel somewhere else for clients?

2) Are your fees affordable for the area where your practice is currently located?

3) Are your fees in line with the services you offer?

4) How many other lawyers in your immediate area may be attempting to pull clients from the same market?

These answers will vary greatly from lawyer to lawyer, however it's still possible to offer guidance.

If you're in an area that truly needs your services and surrounded by people who can afford them then you're in the right market area, even if there are other lawyers in the area who have practices similar to yours.

But if you're located in an area that doesn't truly have a need for your services, or has a need that won't (or can't) be sustained and/or your services are overpriced for that location then you need to re-evaluate your market area. This will hold true even if there are no other lawyers in your area with practices similar to yours.

In a digital age your market doesn't necessarily need to exist in your immediate area but your legal marketing efforts need to exist and be targeted towards those who make up your market. This means that you need to know where they are, or are likely to be. This is especially true if they are not in the neighborhood where you practice.

You know now:

* Who you should be marketing to.

* If the people you should be marketing to are located where you're practicing.

You're now considering:

* What will appeal to your market.

Exercise: Look at your business card and/or marketing piece. Will it appeal to the clients you're trying to attract with your marketing? Are there any changes you can think of that would make it more appealing?

How you should be marketing?

You need to be aware of what appeals to your market and focus on that in your legal marketing efforts. Think about it this way, Starbucks sells more than coffee-based drinks, however when was the last time you saw an advertisement for Starbucks that featured something other than a coffee-based drink? Chances are good that you can't remember a time when this was the case. And if you can, it's a safe bet that there was an advertisement for their coffees or something similar in the same vicinity. This is because Starbucks knows what appeals to their general market.

What do you think will appeal to your market?

Be specific but not too specific. In a later chapter[6] we will focus on branding more heavily and it will be necessary to revisit this. Your answer may change but that's okay.

You know now:

* The importance of following the lead of Starbucks and finding what it is that appeals your particular market.

You're now considering:

* How to appeal to that market.

Try this: http://www.footprintlive.com/ The website acts as an add-on to Google Analytics and can track things such as visitor paths. This will give you better insight into your market from a digital perspective as it'll show you the search terms being used, as well as where visitors to your website are coming from.[7]

Knowing your competitors

Having worked at identifying your market, it is now time to identify your competitors. You're not competing with every other lawyer in your area. You're not even competing with every other lawyer in your area who advertises having a similar practice. Think about it this way: canned spaghetti isn't really comparable to fresh pasta from a 5-star restaurant; similarly if you're in real estate law and you deal solely with residential clients your market isn't the same as a real estate lawyer that deals only with commercial clients.

It's not possible for you to know the exact market of your competitors, but you can certainly get a feel for who they're marketing to. Take a day or two to look at the websites and advertisements for the lawyers in your area who have the same general specialization as you do. After you've done that, it's now possible to classify the sites in one of three categories. Each of these categories has different attributes and will require you to deal with them separately.

Category 1: Practices that don't target your market

These are practices that operate outside of your market. Their clients aren't the same clients that you're looking to work with and/or their specialties are different.

Practices in this category have the following characteristics:

* They don't specialize in the type of law you specialize in.

* They cater to a completely different demographic than your practice caters to.

Category 2: Practices that might target your market

These are practices that may have the same market as you. Some of the potential clients may overlap and/or the practices may have multiple specialties.[8]

Practices in this category have the following characteristics:

* They share your specialization in a broad sense i.e. you both handle patent law.

---

7   Additional information about this site is available in the Resources section.

* They have or are looking to attract the same types of clients that you have or are looking to attract.

Category 3: Practices that share your market

These are the practices that clearly share your market. It's possible that their advertising copy reads like it could be for your practice or you may know firsthand that these lawyers have clients similar to the ones that you're hoping to attract with your legal marketing.

* They share your specialization in a specific sense i.e. you're both immigration lawyers that work closely with Eastern Europeans.

* They have or are looking to attract the same types of clients that you have or are looking to attract.

The practices that are in category 1 aren't your concern.[9] Your focus should be on the practices that make up categories 2 and 3.

Congratulations you've now isolated your current competitors.[10]

You know now:

* How to identify your competitors.

* Who your competitors are.

* That your competitors may change.

---

8   You may find that there are a fair to large number of these types of practices if you're an independent lawyer and you work in an area with a lot of firms.

9   However if they expand into your specialty area they may become category 2 or category 3 practices.

10   Every time a new law practice opens in your area you should take the time to place them into one of the three categories. You may want to create a physical folder or a file on your computer.

* That every lawyer in your area is not competition. Some of these lawyers may even prove to be allies.[11]

You're now considering

* How to work with your competitors.

Exercise: Find business cards and other marketing materials of the law firms that fall into category three.[12] Look at their websites as well. Is there anything that stands out to you? Are there any elements that may appeal strongly to your market? Are there any elements that you think may not appeal to your market at all?

Knowing your market pt. 2: Learning from marketing

Marketing isn't a new concept. Lawyer marketing isn't a new concept. Therefore it's important that you don't try to re-invent the wheel. In later chapters we'll discuss carving your own niche[13] and ways to differentiate yourself from your competition[14] but that's only half the battle. The other half is being willing to learn from what's already happened.

Identifying marketing failures

The only thing more crushing than a marketing failure is a marketing failure that could have been avoided. While it may be hard to find out about past failures since they're not something people tend to brag about, if it was a big enough disaster it would have made the news.

---

11   There will be more on this in chapter 6.

12   All of this information may be available online.

13   Chapter 2.

14   Chapter 4.

This is also a good time to think outside of the box and look not just at the past marketing failures of the legal community but also to consider any missteps that may have occurred elsewhere within the market that you're reaching out to. For example, if your market is bilingual you may want to be extra mindful of issues that can occur when putting out marketing materials in their native language; specifically if you personally don't speak another language you may want to consider either only marketing in English or hiring a reputable translation service.

Take some time and think about the following:

1) Are there any legal or general marketing failures that you remember in relation to your target market?

2) Are there any mistakes that you've personally seen in general advertisements targeted at your market?

3) Are there any words or images that you may want to avoid in your marketing because they've caused controversy in your market in the past?

You know now:

* That when looking for marketing failures you need to look beyond the legal field to anything that may affect your market.

* To be aware of any major mistakes that your competitors have made in the past.

* To avoid words and images that may cause controversy in your market.

You're now considering

* How to avoid similar failures.

Exercise 1: Is there anything about your business card or marketing material that may be seen as being controversial to your market in particular? Is there anything about it that reminds you of something from a company or law practice that failed to successfully market to your core audience?

Exercise 2: Compile a list of words and images that you want to avoid when marketing to your desired clients. Consider things that they'd think of as being offensive or out of touch with who they are.

Turning a failure into a success

Something that begins as a failure doesn't have to end that way. If your current marketing isn't making the right kind of impact, it may be possible for you to not only learn from your own mistakes but also to take those failures and turn them into successes. As an example of this consider the company LifeLock. In order to promote the product, the company's CEO Todd Davis used his own social security number in ad campaigns promoting LifeLock's identity theft prevention service. His social security number was stolen and used to make purchases. For some companies that would have been the end, but not for LifeLock which took these thefts and turned them into a promotional tool showing the service did do it's job by alerting Davis of the fraud so his credit wasn't harmed. The point is that failure can happen to anyone. How you deal with failure is the real test.

Identifying market successes

In addition to educating yourself about past failures you also need to know about the past successes of your competitors. While you don't want to replicate what someone else is doing, there may be certain elements that you can incorporate into your own legal marketing efforts. A good example of incorporation without replication can be seen in car insurance commercials. All of the major care insurance companies use humor as a way to get their messages across but they all do it in a way that's unique to them. Similarly if you notice that all of your competitors utilize a certain color scheme in their marketing you may want to incorporate similar tones in your own marketing. Take some time and think about the following:

1) Are there any legal marketing successes that you remember?

2) Are there any general marketing successes that you remember from ads targeted at your market?

3) Are there any words or images that you may want to include in your marketing because they're being repeated in the advertising targeting your market?

4) Are there any topical issues or trends that are being talked about by your market that you can incorporate into your advertising?

You know now:

      * To be aware of any major successes that your competitors have had in the past.

      * To incorporate words and images that may appeal to your market.

      * To look for new market trends that may equal market success.

You're now considering:

      * How to make past successes work for your current practice.

* How to take current information and turn it into success

Exercise 1: Is there anything about your business card or marketing material that's similar to successful marketing pieces?

<u>Signs of success</u>

Don't make the mistake of confusing stagnation with success. Just because marketing has gone unchanged doesn't mean that it's working. There are numerous reasons why bad marketing remains. Consider that the person producing it may be unwilling or unable to change it. You don't want to model any of your marketing efforts from something stale, so you need to know how to tell the difference between marketing strategies that remain because they've been successful versus those that are stuck in a rut.

Successful marketing will occasionally be revamped to reflect current times and trends while still remaining true to its core message. Stagnant marketing will be dated and more importantly ineffective at getting the attention of the desired market.

Next: Carving Your Niche

Chapter 3: Carving Your Niche

You're a lawyer clearly. But what kind of a lawyer are you? The ability to answer this question and answer it honestly is key in moving forward and making the right kind of impact on your market. You need to make sure that in your legal marketing efforts that you're not only appealing to the people who'll utilize your services, but that you're being true to who you are and the brand that you're looking to build.[15] What's the best way to do this? By identifying your particular niche and knowing its importance. In doing this there are four key things which you need to keep in mind:

* The importance of knowing who you are.

* The importance of knowing what you're selling.

* The importance of creating a niche and not a trap.

* The importance of mastering a specialty.

By the end of this chapter you'll be able to do all of the following:

* Identify who you are as a lawyer.

* Identify what exactly it is you're selling.

* Identify what you should and shouldn't be doing in regards to your personal niche.

What you'll need for this chapter:

* Your business card.

*A pencil and a piece of paper or an empty computer file.

---

15   There will be more in depth information on branding in the following chapter.

Finding a niche

Finding a niche can be as simple as basic addition. Your target audience + your personality + your specialty = your niche.

Your target audience is defined as your market. This is something which was discussed in depth in the previous chapter.

Your personality encompasses who you are and what you're willing to do.

Your specialty is your area of expertise.

Both, personality and specialty will be discussed at length in the pages that follow.

As a basic example of this formula at work, consider it in relation to my practice.

1. Target Audience: All individuals with money, property or other assets, which are not currently being secured in the best way.

2. Personality: An innovator and educator who's very social and very serious about the importance of financial protection.

3. Specialty: Asset protection.

4. My Niche: An asset protection lawyer with the ability to provide both domestic and international Asset Protection plans for clients with any asset size.

By the end of this chapter you should be able to complete this formula for yourself.

The importance of knowing who you are

What kind of a lawyer are you? Your immediate response may be to answer with your specialty. You may answer, "I'm a patent lawyer" or "I'm a criminal attorney." But that isn't specific enough. Think about it this way, all divorces aren't the same thus all divorce lawyers can't be the same. The same logic is true for every area of law and therefore for every lawyer.

While the type of law you practice is a factor, it shouldn't be the only thing that you consider when you're attempting to find your niche. You need to ask yourself some questions about your personality. Keep in mind that these are things that you may not have considered before in terms of your practice.

What type of person are you?

This question is incredibly broad. It's broad for a reason. Because it's broad you're able to include as little or as much information as you think is important. Take some time to consider things you'd probably never consider when you're thinking about your practice or the way to market it. If necessary ask yourself some preliminary questions. Here are a few examples:

1) What do you do for fun?

2) What types of people do you like to spend time with?

3) What do you find stressful?

4) How do you feel about social situations?

Remember that these questions are just examples. They may feel too personal, or maybe even not personal enough. Treat them as a starting off point and know that you can add some questions that you think would be more useful, get rid of questions that you don't like or create a set of questions that's completely different. You may even want to ask someone else to come up with a few questions for you and answer them instead.

Feel free to think about this. Really consider the main question: What type of a person are you? If necessary take a few hours, or even a day or two. But don't move forward until you feel sure of the answer. Accepting who you are as a person is key to integrating your individuality into your practice.

As an asset protection lawyer it's imperative that my clients know they can trust me to do what's going to be best for them so my demeanor needs to show them that they can. And it does. I'm open about the fact that I've worked in other fields, that I've been an entrepreneur and that I respect what it takes to make money and the importance of keeping that money secure. My past has been able to work to my advantage in the present by providing my particular practice with credibility. I don't advise my clients on how to be prepared in the face of potential financial danger; I prepare them for what to do when it happens. I believe in being proactive and professional while always remembering that personal setbacks are a part of life.

What does your demeanor say to your clients? How do you incorporate your personality into your practice?

You know now:

* That an important part of carving your niche is knowing who you are as an individual.

* The importance of looking beyond your practice to add personality to your legal marketing.

You're now considering:

* Which aspects of your personality you incorporate into your practice.

Try this: http://www.humanmetrics.com/cgi-win/jtypes2.asp

This website will provide you with an online personality test. It'll help if you get stuck trying to answer the question regarding who you are as a person.[16]

Exercise: In a clear and concise sentence write out what your personality is.

The importance of knowing what you're selling

You may think that as a lawyer what you're selling are your services. And that's correct. But it's not complete. As a lawyer you're not just selling the service of your counsel. You're also selling your particular skill set, reputation and attitude. The combination of all these things together can be considered as your specialty.

I'm sure that you have a favorite restaurant or store. Chances are good that the restaurant serves a type of food that can be found other places or that the store carries products that you could get somewhere else. But there's something about that particular restaurant or store that appeals to you. Maybe it's the customer service, or the prices or even the location. Whatever it is, there's at least one reason why you rank this place as being your favorite. This isn't an accident. These places know that

---

16   This personality test is not meant to be used as a full assessment of who you are. Think of it as a creative tool that may give you some insight.

they're not just selling their food or their products but that those things are a part of a larger package.

It's important that you think about your practice in the same way. Is your counsel important? Certainly. Equally important though is the way in which you present what it is that you do. With this thought in mind there are three questions that you need to ask yourself. Take some time to really think about the answers.

1) How would you describe your practice to someone who had no idea what you did for a living?

2) How would you describe your practice to someone who knew you were a lawyer?

3) How would you describe your practice to someone who knew you were a lawyer and knew your specialty?

Go back and look at your three answers. Are the descriptions accurate? Is there anything you can add? Is there anything you should take away? Most importantly, are all three answers the same?

Hint: They should be.[17]

You've identified your market so what you're selling should be consistent no matter who you have to describe it to.

If your answers are consistent, great. It means that you have a good grip on what you're putting out into the market which means you have a better chance of getting the returns that you want.

---

17   The answers may not be the same word for word but you should be conveying the same core message.

If your answers aren't consistent you need to do some additional evaluation. Is your tone different? Is your language different? Is your message different? Why? Work on your message so that no matter who you're sharing it with it says the same thing.

You know now:

* You're not just selling your services. You're selling you.

* A consistent message.

You're now considering:

* Ways to ensure that your message remains consistent no matter who you're sharing it with.

Exercise: Take a look at your business card. Does it look like the business card of someone who's trying to sell what you're selling? What about it will help a prospective client understand what you're selling? What about it will make a prospective client feel comfortable working with you? What about it may confuse a prospective client? Is there anything about it that may make a prospective client feel uncomfortable about doing business with you?

What not to do pt. 1: Putting yourself in a box

Anyone who has ever seen a mime is familiar with them pretending to be trapped in a box. Don't trap yourself in a box by pretending that it's *your* niche. If you're not comfortable with certain things or haven't mastered them but you act like you are or you have, you may find yourself in a situation where clients expect things from you that you're not willing to or able to provide.

Think about how successful Lady Gaga is. Part of that comes from the crazy outfits she wears. Part of it comes from her publicity. And part of it is certainly her music. She fills a very specific niche, an eccentric artist that's unafraid of being a brand and regularly interacts with her fans. Now imagine if in the middle of a tour she started doing shows in jeans and t-shirts. It'd be shocking. And because it occurred so suddenly, fans would probably feel cheated.

That's the same feeling your clients would have if you haven't been honest about who you are and what you're selling. That's not the impression that you want to make.

You know now:

* That you shouldn't attempt to fake your way into a niche.

You're now considering:

* The importance of being honest about what you can and are willing to provide.

Exercise: Look critically at your business card. Is it a good representation of your niche? Consider ways to improve it to be a more solid representation of the role you want to fill as a lawyer.

What not to do pt. 2: Being a jack of all trades

You're probably familiar with the title "Jack of all trades, master of none". That's precisely who you don't want to be. Sure that's the guy or girl who may initially seem like they're getting all the work and some clients may even be drawn to the fact that they have multiple specialties. But it's an act that gets really old, really fast. And in the long run you're not going to make any money or be truly trusted by quality clients that will continually utilize your services.

I'm sure that if you had to go to a doctor for surgery on your foot that you'd choose an orthopedic surgeon who'd performed similar surgeries hundreds of times before rather than a general practitioner who'd performed the surgery once or twice but also assured you that he could check for colon cancer, do a vision test and whiten your teeth. There's something highly comforting about knowing that the person we're trusting with something important has earned that trust by doing the same thing we need for other people. The same way you wouldn't trust a doctor who didn't have a specialty, you can't expect a potential client to trust you if you refuse to specify what it is that you do.

If you currently have multiple specialties now is the time to narrow them down to a single one. Don't automatically choose one over the others because you think it'll make you more money. Also don't automatically choose one over the others because it's something that you feel idealistic about.

You know now:

* The importance of having a specialization.

* That being a jack of all trades doesn't pay off.

You're now considering:

* What exactly your specialization is.

Exercise 1: In a clear and concise sentence write out what your specialty is.

Exercise 2: Complete the formula for finding a niche.

Your Target audience is _____

Your personality is _____

Your specialty is _____

Your niche is _____

Next: Branding

Chapter 4: Branding

If I were to tell you that Disney, Apple[18] and Christian Louboutin shoes all had something in common you'd probably tell me that I was crazy. Well, I'm not crazy. And I'm telling you that those three things are more related than you think. Disney is home to iconic characters that are recognized internationally. Apple has created an entire ecosystem of products that work together. Christian Louboutin shoes have a red sole that are so recognizable as to become proprietary. All of this is a result of branding. Really amazing branding.

This chapter is separated into five parts, each providing information on how you can build your own brand.

Part one focuses on defining your brand. This entails re-evaluating what it is you're selling, who you're selling it to and ways to appeal to your market.

By the end of part one you'll be able to do all of the following:

* Identify what type of brand you're building.

* Identify what type of marketing messages will appeal to your clients.

Part two focuses on what differentiates your brand from that of other law practices. This will involve looking at the role that your niche will play as well as looking at ways to stand out even further from your competition.

---

18   The computer company. Not the fruit.

By the end of part two you'll be able to do all of the following:

    * Identify exactly what will make your brand different from other similar lawyers.

    * Identify how far outside of the box you're willing to go in terms of marketing.

Part three focuses on harnessing creativity. This is an incredibly important aspect in a business as old as the legal profession.

    By the end of part three you'll be able to do all of the following:

    * Identify how much creativity your market will tolerate.

    * Identify ways to attract and hire creative talent.

Part four focuses on harnessing uniqueness. While this is related in part to the niche which you've defined, it goes beyond that as it's more about looking for ways to reach out to your market that your competition may not be thinking of.

    By the end of part four you'll be able to do all of the following:

    * Identify a truly unique idea.

    * Identify ways to make your practice unique that will still appeal to your market.

Part five focuses on creating an overall brand identity. It will tie together the previous four parts.

    By the end of part five you'll be able to do the following:

    * Identify your overall brand.

What you'll need for this chapter:

* One of your current business cards.

* The current business card of one of your direct competitors.

* Any additional marketing material you may have.

* Any additional marketing material from the same direct competitor that you have the business card for.

* A pencil and a piece of paper or an empty computer file.

Defining your brand

You may think that as a lawyer you don't necessarily have any need to build a brand. Brands are usually associated with large companies or national products. There are brands of jeans, brands of microwave popcorn, brands of cosmetics and brands of almost anything else you can think of. The concept of branding isn't a new one and it's far more important to your practice than you may be thinking it is right now. Branding is defined as follows:

"The process involved in creating a unique name and image for a product in the consumers' mind, mainly through advertising campaigns with a consistent theme. Branding aims to establish a significant and differentiated presence in the market that attracts and retains loyal customers."[19]

While the whole definition is important there are some definite key words that you should keep in mind. The words "unique," "consistent," "significant," and "differentiated" should immediately stand

---

19   Definition provided by http://www.businessdictionary.com. The specific link is http://www.businessdictionary.com/definition/branding.html.

out. This is because no matter what your final brand image is, it should incorporate all of those elements.

What's your brand

Whether you realize it or not you've been building your brand since the moment you began practicing law. Clients, potential clients and even your competition has looked at you, your business cards and your attitude for indicators of your brand. If you were aware of this, chances are good that if nothing else your message has been consistent. But if this is news to you then perhaps you haven't behaved in a manner that reflects a cohesive brand identity. That's okay. But from this moment on you have to realize that the same way the look and performance of a car can be seen as a reflection of the overall brand that the way you present yourself and your practice has the same effect.

Earlier chapters have asked you to look at who you are, what you're selling and who you're selling to. Now is the time to put all of these things together. Think about whether or not your answers to those three questions actually work well together. It's important that they do because they'll form the basis for your brand identity. If there are any inconsistencies then they need to be reconciled now. Right now.

Successful brands know the importance of this, and when they attempt to do something that ignores the fact that these elements need to work together they usually end up paying the price for it.

The date April 23, 1985 may not have any special meaning for you but it's a date that Coca-Cola will never be able to forget. It was the day that "new coke" was presented to the public. If you've never heard of "new coke" it's because the product was a major marketing failure. In trying to compete with Pepsi, Coca Cola forgot who they were as a brand as well as the fact that what they were selling needed to appeal first and foremost to the loyal market that had been buying their product for years.

You know now:

     * That your brand should be based on who you are, what you're selling and who you're selling to.

     * That any changes to your brand still need to remain consistent to who you are, what you're selling and who you're selling it to.

You're now considering:

     * Whether or not you have the foundation to build a strong brand.

     * Any changes that can or should be made in order to make who you are and what you're selling more consistent with who you're selling to.

Exercise: Look at your business card critically. Does it look like a good representation of your brand? Is it consistent with your other marketing material? If you removed all of the identifying information i.e. name and phone number, would the pieces look like they came from the same person?

What will appeal to your clients

     What do you think will appeal to your market?

     This question was asked in an earlier chapter and if you haven't already done so, now is the time to come up with an answer. Knowing what you know about your target audience what do you think will get and keep their attention in terms of advertising? Figuring this out may seem like a daunting task but it doesn't have to be. Think back on your last few client interactions.[20] Even without directly saying so your clients are letting you know what's important to them. You just have to be savvy enough to pick up on it. You also have to be willing to remember it. Treat every client interaction as a chance to do market research. Just make sure it doesn't interfere with doing your job.

For instance, if one of your clients drives an older car that isn't an antique but is still in amazing condition then it's likely that he or she prefers something reliable and trusted as opposed to needing what's flashy and new. This is in stark contrast to the client who every time you see them has the latest phone or newest handbag. But, if you're willing to look you can find common threads that link them. Those commonalities are the basis of what will appeal to your market.

Using those same two clients, it can be argued that they're both in search of quality. They simply have different ways of trying to find it. One client holds on to things that have lasted and the other seeks out newer models. Style may be more important to one than it is to the other but they both require a certain amount of substance to be satisfied. Most importantly both of them are willingly coming to you.

Of course the more clients you have, the more difficult it may be for you to find those common threads. But the ability to do so is crucial to your legal marketing efforts. It will allow you to build a brand that caters to your target audience. However make sure that while appealing to your market that you're still being true to yourself.

---

20   No clients yet? No problem. Instead save this information and reference back to it when you begin meeting with clients.

You know now:

    * How to answer the question of what appeals to your market.

    * That while you should appeal to your clients that your brand needs to remain true to you.

You're now considering:

    * How your clients are alike.

Exercise: Write out or use a diagram to draw out information regarding what makes your clients similar. What qualities and traits stand out? How can these qualities and traits be transformed into images?

Try this: https://bubbl.us/. This website will allow you to brainstorm online. It may be more effective than a sheet of paper and a pencil and will allow you to visually map out the commonalities between your clients.

Differentiating your brand

The number of lawyers in each state are greater than the need for lawyers in each state.[21] For this reason, above many others, it's important that as a lawyer your brand is appealing to the market that you share with your competition. It's also highly important that potential clients have no trouble in figuring out what makes you different and why being different equals being better equipped to handle their legal needs.

<u>What makes your brand different</u>

Nike, Reebok and Adidas are all brands of sneakers. They use similar materials, similar colors and all have access to athletes and

---

21   This is according to a 2011 article entitled "The Lawyer Surplus, State by state" http://economix.blogs.nytimes.com/2011/06/27/the-lawyer-surplus-state-by-state/.

celebrities in terms of promoting their products. But they're not the same. And they're not marketed the same way. Think about the ads that you've seen for each company, whether they were in print, on television or online. The products being offered shared similarities but there was something unique about each one being conveyed in the message. This is true of all products. Each energy drink, every bar of soap and every travel booking website does something a little different from their competition in order to appeal to the market that they share. The same should be true for you as a lawyer.

What makes you different from every other lawyer you're competing against?

In the previous chapter I showed you a formula for finding your niche. That formula holds the answer to what it is that makes you different. Yes, you share a target audience with other lawyers and your specialty may be similar but your personality is uniquely yours. And it can be used in order to help you stand out. You are your brand. So it only makes sense that you should serve as the means of making your brand stand out from all of the others.

You know now:

* That similar products are not sold in the exact same way therefore similar lawyers don't need to brand in the same way.

* That you are the key to helping your brand stand out. Your personality is what makes you different.

You're now considering:

   * Ways to incorporate your personality more fully into your practice and translate it into your marketing.

Exercise: Look at your business cards and marketing material alongside those of one of your direct competitors. Are they too similar?[22] Does your business card have any of your personality in it? If it does, is it enough? Is it too much? If it doesn't, how can you incorporate it?

How far are you willing to go

   Sex sells. It's why ads are filled with good-looking people, often in as little clothes as plausible. Controversy also sells. It's why reality t.v. and tabloids are so popular. But just because these things are known to make money and known to appeal to massive audiences, it doesn't mean that they make sense for you or your brand.

   Think about the following questions:

1) How edgy are you?

2) How far outside the box are you willing to take your branding?

3) How well do you handle conflict and controversy?

4) Could you handle potentially losing a large share of your market?

   There are no right or wrong answers to these questions. But you have to be honest with yourself and honest about who your market is.

   You may be edgy and willing to be incredibly over the top in terms of your marketing efforts but if you don't like conflict or could be out of a job if half your market walked away then you want to stay away from anything that's going to be too polarizing.

If you're insistent about pushing the envelope then start small. Test the waters with a short run ad offline and see how it's received. For example if you're a family lawyer with younger clients looking for paternity tests or dealing with custody disputes you may approach local single spots with condoms in custom printed packages with the slogan "Just in case they aren't "THE ONE" with your web address on the bottom.[23] Such tactics may work wonders but they may also backfire or not have any real effect at all so you have to be prepared either way.

You know now:

* That just because something works for one market doesn't mean that it'll work for your market.

* That you need to honestly assess both how different you want to be and what your market will tolerate.

* That if you want to push boundaries initially do it in a way that's small.

You're now considering:

* What your personal limits are in terms of being different.

Exercise: Look at the websites or marketing materials of three of your direct competitors. Can you spot any differences between them? Are the

---

22   While there may be certain similarities i.e. a similar color scheme which has proven successful with your market they shouldn't look like they could be from the same firm.

23   To the best of my knowledge this hasn't been done by a lawyer.

differences subtle or obvious? What can you do to your own marketing materials and website to make them stand out from this group?

Harnessing Creativity

Imagine for a moment a world where every car was a four door sedan that came in either navy blue or black; a world where every television set was exactly 36 inches and every restaurant had the exact same food prepared in the exact same way with no variations or substitutions. If you grew up in such a place it would seem perfectly normal but since you didn't I bet it seems bland. You don't want your brand to be bland.

What will your market tolerate

While every market has its limits regarding what it'll tolerate there are ways to work within those limits to help your brand stand out.

As an example of this consider my business cards. My business cards were designed to look like credit cards at first glance. They're also made of the same plastic so they feel like credit cards as well. Because they look like something familiar people respond well to them.[24] They're also more likely to keep them because the cards are unique. I chose a creative way to show my clients and potential clients that I was personally in touch with wealth and I did it in a way that was elegant but still powerful, a way that resonated with my market.

No matter who your target audience is there's a way to be creative that captures their attention as opposed to turning them off. For example, if you're an environmental attorney your marketing materials can be made

---

24   And are more likely to pick them up.

from recycled paper. Additionally you may want to eliminate paper altogether and use things such as electronic business cards instead.[25] Revisit and re-evaluate some of what was discussed earlier in the book; are there any past successes that you can re-imagine to create a new campaign?

You know now:

    * That creative efforts need to be in line with your overall brand.

    * That your creative efforts need to entice and not alienate your target audience.

You're now considering:

    * Ways to incorporate creative elements into your marketing that will work with your market.

Try this: http://www.plastekcards.com/. This website features plastic business cards. Such cards are a durable and memorable alternative to more standard paper cards.

Hiring creative talent

You may be saying to yourself that you're not creative. You're a lawyer, and a good one not a graphic designer or website builder. That's okay. There are numerous places you can go to hire creative talent. You can check out graphic designers in your local area, ask friends and family for recommendations or try one of the following websites:

    * https://www.elance.com. This is a free website that allows you to post jobs or browse professionals by skill set.

---

25   See the resources section for information on electronic business card options.

* http://www.craigslist.com/. This is the main page for Craigslist and will lead you to any of the branches of the site based on state first.

* http://fiverr.com/. This website specializes in getting projects done for the fee of $5. The graphics and advertising sections are good places to start.

* http://99designs.com/. This website allows you launch design contests for graphic art such as book covers, websites, business cards, banner ads, illustrations, and more. You pay a flat fee upfront and designers will submit designs for a specified period of time. You can critique and eliminate designs as you go along. In the end, you pick a winner and personalize your design to your satisfaction with that winner. Once everything is done, you obtain the design files from the winning designer.

Harnessing Uniqueness

There are no truly unique ideas. There are however unique ways of implementing ideas. It's important to remember this when you're thinking about your brand. *How* you convey a message is of equal importance to what is being conveyed.

Think about this in terms of the music industry. If you listen closely to country music and rap music you'll note a number of similar themes. Don't believe me? Consider the similarities between rap music and country music, specifically between Loretta Lynn and Nicki Minaj. Both have at least one song that focuses on the theme of being in some way better than someone else, specifically another woman. While the songs are clearly for different audiences, it's unmistakable that they're playing to the same type of mentality. This is a great example of how different markets can respond to similar messages based on delivery.

You know now:

    * That there are no unique ideas but there are unique ways of sharing them.

    * That how you say something is as important as what you're saying.

You're now considering:

    * Ways to make your message stand out among a sea of similar messages.

Exercise: Take the sentence "I'm the best lawyer in the world." Think about how you would communicate that to various markets. How would you present that information to different people? Would the structure of the sentence be changed? Would the delivery method be changed i.e. would you text it for one group and place it on billboards for another? How would you communicate this sentence to your target market.

Creating an overall brand identity

    Branding isn't a buzzword. It's a foundation that you have to build and continuously cultivate. Only after you've acknowledged what you can offer as an individual you can begin to grow into your overall brand identity.

    You need to think about what you're saying, how you're saying it, who you're saying it to and why anyone should listen to you over your competitors. These things need to be questions you can immediately respond to and integrate into every part of your practice.

Next: Becoming an Expert

Chapter 5: Becoming an Expert

When you hear the word expert there are certain things that you expect of the person whose been given that label. You expect them to know about their field and you generally trust them because their reputation reflects behavior that says they deserve it. But when you hear the word do you think about yourself? Do you look in the mirror and see an expert? If you don't, then no one else will. And you want everyone to see an expert when they look at you, after you've put in a lot of work to earn that title.

This chapter is separated into two parts.

The first part focuses on ways that you can build your credibility. Being viewed as credible is crucial to gaining expert status.

By the end of part one you'll be able to do all of the following:

* Identify what your specific expertise is.

* Identify four key ways in which you can share your expertise.

The second part focuses on maintaining your expert status. Even after you begin to be viewed as an expert, it will be necessary for you to reinforce that status in ways that work for you and not against you.

By the end of part two you'll be able to do all of the following:

* Identify the difference between selling your services and sharing your knowledge.

* Realize the importance of a consistent message.

What you'll need for this chapter:

* One of your current business cards.

* A pencil and a piece of paper or an empty computer file.

* A tape recorder or microphone and sound recorder program.[26]

* Your calendar or planner.[27]

* An internet connection.

Building your credibility

Building your credibility is about two things. And without both of them it's impossible to do. First you need to figure out what your expertise is. Then you need to share what it is you know in a public way.

<u>What's your expertise</u>

Remember back in chapter 2 we discussed carving a niche? The formula for finding your niche involved identifying your specialty, your particular area of expertise. This wasn't only a key part of that formula, it's also necessary for moving forward now.

If you couldn't quite answer that question then, now is the time for you to truly consider it. If you're having trouble doing this try asking yourself the following questions:

1) What area of law are you currently practicing?

2) Is there anything special about the way in which you practice?[28]

3) Is there anything special about the knowledge you have?[29]

---

26 Even if you've never used it, your computer probably has a basic sound recorder program. If for whatever reason your computer doesn't, you can download an open source program such as Audacity for free http://audacity.sourceforge.net/.

27 This can be an online or hard copy version just make sure that it's up to date.

28 If necessary go back to Chapter 1, Knowing Your Market, for inspiration on how to answer this.

If you were able to answer that question, there are also some things for you to consider. First consider how honest the answer was. Also think about how compatible it is with your personality. Your area of expertise is something that you will need to live and breathe in order for it to be believable and that means that it should be something that you're genuinely interested in and is aligned with who you are.

Think about it this way if you have something that you're truly passionate about there's a good chance that you can talk about it at almost any time to almost any one without hesitation. Now imagine having to do the same thing with something that you're not passionate about. While you may be able to discuss it sometimes, there's a good chance that eventually you'll grow to hate the subject because you're being forced to repeat something that you don't really believe in.

You know now:

* That you need to be passionate about whatever your expertise is in.

You're now considering:

* Whether or not the specialty you identified in chapter 2 is the expertise that you want to move forward with.

Exercise: Fill in the following statement without hesitation: "My expertise is _____."

Answer this question now. Answer it again tomorrow. And the day after. Repeat this process for a full week. If your answer changes ask

---

29   This includes anything that may be considered proprietary or any tips that you've picked up and are willing to share.

yourself, why? Are there common elements between your answers? Are you honestly more passionate about one than the other?

<u>Sharing your expertise</u>

Having identified your area of expertise, it's now necessary for you to find ways for you to share what you know. This goes beyond word of mouth or a few scattered activities. You need to develop a plan of action that is both in line with your market and manageable.

Chapter 1 focused on knowing your market. Revisit your notes from that chapter and remember that it's important to always keep in mind what appeals to your market and what will turn them off. This may mean that you need to slightly alter the ways in which you share your expertise. These alterations will be related to the style and not the delivery method.

Having taken your market into consideration you also need to consider your own schedule. You want to be sure that you have enough time to work on whatever you have planned. This statement is as true for your practice and the clients you represent as it is for any projects that you'll be working on to attract them. Don't begin anything that you don't feel confident that you'll be able to complete. You don't want to develop the reputation of being a flake when in reality you're just over scheduled.

You know now:

* That your plan of action for building credibility has to make sense for your market and your schedule.

You're now considering:

* How much extra activity your schedule can handle.

Exercise: Look critically at your calendar or planner. Are there a lot of commitments already listed? Are you able to move any of them or realistically work around them? Don't just think about what else you can add to your schedule and complete but rather what else you can add and complete well. If there aren't a lot of commitments listed consider why this is the case. Have you intentionally given yourself a lot of free time or is that time that you would willingly fill with other activity? If the free time is intentional you may only want to attempt one credibility building activity so that you devote to it the attention it deserves.

There are four key ways in which you can work towards building the credibility to be considered an expert. These include writing articles and books, teaching classes, speaking at seminars and creating valuable content that can be easily accessed. All of these activities may not work for you. That's okay. Look at the information provided for each and then decide.

<u>Writing articles and books</u>

Why are you reading this book? It could just be a matter of wanting to be a better marketer for your legal practice. It could be that you were intrigued by the contents. But I'm sure that my credentials didn't hurt. The fact that I'm still a practicing lawyer probably resonated with you on some level. And that's part of the point. Just as you may have chosen this book because of my background, there are people who'll read articles and books because they're interested in gaining information from someone with your expertise.

Before you can begin writing you need to first think about what it is that you have to say. And if you have enough words to say it with accuracy and authority. Don't feel the need to immediately create a masterpiece. Expect that you'll spend some time working on drafts. And most importantly, don't get discouraged if at first things don't go as smoothly as you immediately assumed they would. Here are some factors that you need to keep in mind.

* Who are you writing for?

Are you writing for your clients or creating something for your peers? The tone and delivery style will be different based on your intended audience. You'll want to be aware of things such as the language that you're choosing, the final length and what you're looking to convey. Each of these elements will be important in creating a final product that's worthy of putting your name on, something that you'll want associated with you and your practice. Think about it this way, if you're looking for a genuine children's book you're not going to pick up a book that's a clear parody. While they're the right length for a bedtime story and feature illustrations fitting for a picture book, they're also often sarcastic and cynical and are better suited to new parents or old friends who may have enjoyed the original. You need to be as clear when it comes to what you're writing. There should be no question regarding who your article or book is geared towards.

* What are you going to write about?

You've honed in on your area of expertise and now is the time for you to focus even further. Think about all of the books out there that deal with your practice in some way. Is there an element in fiction books featuring legal practices like yours that simply isn't true? Is there something new or interesting that you can add to what's already available in the non-fiction section? Are you looking to reach an audience that's being ignored? It's important that you ask yourself questions like these in order to get an idea regarding what you'd like to write about. Note that it may be helpful to write out or draw out your ideas so feel free to brainstorm; write, type or sketch any initial ideas that come to mind.

* Where do you want to see your work?

If you're expecting to see your article appear in the *New York Times* or assuming that your book will end up in Barnes and Nobles then you're not being realistic. While it's completely possible that something you write may end up getting some press that you didn't anticipate but you're a lawyer and not a full-time author so you should keep your expectations much more focused. When asking yourself this question, be sure to think about your intended audience. If you're working on an article to help your clients then a realistic answer to this question could involve wanting to see your writing where it'll be easily accessible to your market. In that same vein, if you're writing something geared towards law students, it's a realistic goal to want to see your work in classrooms.

* When will you find time to write?

Do you honestly have time in your schedule that will allow you to write? This isn't a question that anyone else can answer for you. You know what your schedule is like, what your habits are and whether or not you'll have time to finish a project once it's started. If your practice is busy it may be beneficial for you to begin with an article or two before committing to anything longer.

* Why are you writing?

The answer to this question shouldn't be "to build my credibility as an expert." While that's certainly a part of it, this shouldn't be your only reason for writing. If you're not interested in the subject matter, there's a good chance that whatever you create won't be interesting to your readers. Consider why it is that you've decided to write and *infuse* that into your final piece. For example, if you're looking to be informative make sure that you're offering information that your audience needs.

* How are you going to make this information available?

Are you planning on writing articles to post on your website or are you looking to submit them to law journals? Will you be selling your book or giving it away? The answers to these questions should in no way effect the quality of your work but it is possible that they will effect your schedule differently. For instance, if you're writing articles that will be posted on your personal site, or publishing a book on your own you can control the timing differently than if they'll be a part of a larger work produced by someone else or if you're being paid to produce the content. It'll be necessary to revisit your schedule to see what type of writing is realistic for you.

* Is writing something you can do?

The ability to put together a sentence doesn't make you a writer any more than the ability to cook a meal makes you a chef. Do a bit of personal assessment and consider whether or not writing is something that you can actually do. If you find that you're not cut out for writing realize that there are other things that you can legitimately do in order to see your name in print. This includes collaborating on an article or a book or hiring a ghostwriter who will write for you. In both instances you would provide information and assist as necessary and someone else would handle the work of actually writing the book out.

You know now:

* That your first attempt at writing may not go smoothly.

* That you need to be clear about who your audience is.

* That you need to be clear about your topic.

* That it's important to know when you'll have time to write.

* That you should have an idea of where you want to see your work.

* That you need to know how you plan on making what you write available.

* That it's possible to collaborate with someone else or to hire a ghostwriter.

You're now considering:

* Who you're going to be writing for.

* What information you can offer your audience.

* Where you want to see your work.

* Whether or not you will be writing alone or with the help of someone else.

Exercise: Visit the website http://750words.com/.[30] Go there and do a free write on the first topic that comes to mind. It doesn't have to be

---

30   More information on this site is available in the resources section.

related to your practice or even to the legal field, just write what comes to mind. How did you feel about writing? Did it feel natural? Did it feel strained? Wait a day and visit the website again. This time write about your practice, any aspect of it is fine. How did you feel this time? Wait another day and visit the website for a third time. This time think about your audience and write something that you think will appeal to them. Look over what you wrote critically. Would it make a good article? Could it be fleshed out into a book? If not, think about what could make it better.

Try this: http://ezinearticles.com/. Once you have written your first article this website will allow you to upload it.

Try this: http://www.BrooklinePress.com/. This is a good resource if you wish to deal with a boutique publisher.

Teaching classes

While teachers don't have to be experts in their fields, enthusiastic experts can make amazing teachers. Could you make an amazing teacher? I'm not suggesting a career change but rather suggesting that one of the best ways to be seen as an authority, is by putting yourself in a position where you are the authority.

* Who do you want to teach?

Are you better with adults or adolescents? Do you want an audience that has some knowledge about what you plan to inform them about or do you want an audience that is completely novice? These are just some of the questions that you need to be asking yourself when you're thinking about who you want to teach. You're in the unique position of being able to select your core audience. Take advantage of that by really thinking about the group that would benefit the most from what you have to offer and the group that you'd best be able to identify with.

* What will you teach?

You have to have a plan of action. And that plan of action needs to be realistic. You're not going to have an unlimited amount of time in which to convey your message so you will need to be clear about what that message is before you set foot in the classroom. While there may be deviations from your lesson plans due to discussions that go longer than expected or similar situations, you'll need to actually have a lesson plan in place. Think about what information you can offer that isn't currently being offered, or consider existing courses that you may be able to expand on. Make sure that no matter what you choose that it's a subject that you can speak about with clarity and passion.

* Where do you want to teach?

Just as all students aren't the same, all classroom environments aren't the same, either. While you may be able to spark stimulating conversation anywhere, certain locations may not be the best choice for you. Do you want a location that's close to your office or are you willing to travel? Depending on where you're located that may be the difference between teaching in a community college setting or an adult education center. Do you want to be in a certain neighborhood? Are you anticipating that the people in your legal market will also be your audience for this venture? These things will play a role in where you're able to teach so be sure to consider them carefully and know that you may have to prioritize which factors are more important than others.

* When will you find time to teach?

You're a lawyer, not a professor, and finding the time to teach may not immediately resonate as a priority but it's something you should think about seriously before looking for or accepting a teaching position. If late nights and long days are a regular part of your schedule traditional teaching may not be an avenue you'll be able to consider but there are ways around that. Consider offering classes on an online platform such as http://moodle.com/. Moodle is a free service that allows anyone to put together a course and offer it.[31] Setting up the class in such a way is something that should work with any schedule.

* Why are you teaching?

You need to want to teach for more reasons than the fact that it may look good on your resume or boost your reputation. While those are great benefits, they aren't the reasons you should be focused on. Think back to your own school days, chances are good you had at least one teacher who you could tell really loved his or her job and at least one teacher who was probably only there because of tenure. You want to be like the teacher who really loved his or her job so think of as many reasons as you can for why you want to be in front of the classroom.

* How are you going to teach?

Are you extroverted and looking to engage the entire room or are you more interested in providing as much information as possible? The only right answer to that question is the one that best aligns with your personality. Your teaching style is going to play a big role in the energy in

---

31   More information on Moodle is available in the resources section.

your classroom. You need to think about if you want to be more animated or more reserved and whether or not what you want to teach will fit in with the style that you've selected.

You know now:

    * That you need to be clear about who you want to teach.

    * That you need to be clear about what you want to teach.

    * That it's important to know where you want to teach.

    * That you don't have to teach in a traditional classroom setting.

    * That your enthusiasm is important.

    * That your teaching style is important.

You're now considering:

    * Who you want to teach.

    * What information you can offer your audience.

    * Where you want to teach.

    * Whether or not you will be teaching in a traditional or digital setting.

Exercise 1: Imagine that you were offered a teaching assignment today and given a week to prepare your materials. Over the course of the next week list anything that comes to mind that you think would be beneficial for you to provide to your students. Are you considering handouts or in-class demonstrations? Will there be homework? At the end of the week look critically at your list. Are the items on it reasonable? Are they things that you could produce or outsource? Will they appeal to your target audience?

Exercise 2: Take a few days to research locations where you can teach. If you're looking to work with law students, look for law schools in your area that may offer guest teacher positions. If you're looking to work with adults contact adult education facilities in the area and find out the criteria for teaching a class. Make a list of the places that both work for you in terms of location and schedule.

Speaking at seminars

Speaking at seminars can be a great addition or alternative to writing books or teaching classes. While it still involves preparation on your part, there's not as large of a time commitment required. Therefore it may be one of the best ways to build your credibility as an expert when you don't have a lot of free time.

* Who do you want to speak to?

Making the decision regarding who you want to speak to is a highly important one. In thinking about this consider factors such as whether you want to be in a room full of your peers or if you'd prefer to be speaking to students or potential clients.

* What will you say?

You shouldn't accept or inquire about a speaking engagement until you're clear about what it is that you want to say. Are you looking to just be informative or do you want to entertain as well? Are you more comfortable with the formal language of your practice or can you just as easily speak to people who may not know the jargon? Is what you want to talk about something that you could talk for 30 minutes without repeating yourself or potentially boring your audience? Could you last an hour?

Could you handle answering questions on the subject? Make sure you have answers to all of these questions before deciding on what subject you'll speak about.

* Where do you want to speak?

Does the thought of speaking in front of a large crowd terrify? Would you rather have an audience where you could be sure that you could greet everyone individually or do you want to look out and see a group of 100 people? By answering these questions you'll be answering where it is that you truly want to speak. If you like small groups then your speaking locations will be limited to smaller venues. It's important to note though that this doesn't necessarily mean that you'll have less of an impact than someone who chooses to speak to large conventions, it just means that you'll have less of a reach.

* When will you have time to speak?

If you're the head of a large practice or have a large client load, it may not be feasible for you to take off a couple of days or even a few hours to go and do a speaking engagement. This however doesn't mean that you'll be shut off from the benefits that they offer. If you look at your schedule and realize that you don't have time to speak[32] then you should try podcasting.[33] This may prove a viable and effective alternative to the more traditional speaking engagement as it can be done completely on your schedule and allows you to directly market it to your chosen audience.

---

32   Or if the thought of public speaking terrifies you.

33   A podcast is a digital audio or visual file that can be downloaded to a media player or computer from a website.

* Why are you speaking?

Think about what type of void your speaking in public will fill. Are you providing your community or market with information that they may not be getting from elsewhere? Do you have something that you can share with your colleagues? You need to know what your motivations are before you move forward.

* How are you going to book speaking engagements?

Do you handle your own appointments or do you have someone else handling them for you? In either instance you need to be aware that booking a speaking engagement is rarely just as simple as calling someone and sealing the deal. It may require multiple calls and emails before you even speak to someone who can actually book you at their venue. And once the engagement is booked you'll need to be sure that it doesn't conflict with anything else on your schedule. This could be especially challenging if you're a trial lawyer or working as a part of a firm where your schedule fluctuates from week to week.

You know now:

* That you need to be clear about who you want to speak to.

* That you need to be clear about what you want to speak about.

* That it's important to know what type of venue you'd be most comfortable speaking at.

* That you don't have to perform speaking engagements in a traditional manner but can also utilize a digital solution.

* That booking a speaking engagement generally won't be as simple as making a single phone call.

You're now considering:

> * Who you want to speak to.

> * What information you can offer your audience.

> * What type of venue will work best for your personality.

> * Whether or not you can benefit from a digital alternative.

> * Is there anything you can provide to enhance your speaking engagements? Is there any take home information that you can you offer instead of your marketing materials?

Exercise: Make a list of items that you could offer to the people who come to hear you speak. Depending on your chosen audience consider whether something like magnets or brochures would be effective. Also, what would be most cost effective for you to produce?

Try this: www.fullcalendar.com. For a small fee this site will promote your event to a variety of other outlets.[34]

Try this: www.thepodcasthost.com. This is a free podcasting website that will allow you to create, manage and even list your podcast on Itunes.[35]

Try this: www.tungle.me/Home/. This website will help you keep your speaking engagements straight once you begin to book them.

Creating valuable content

You may be thinking that by writing articles or books or by offering items at classes or seminars that you're already providing valuable

---

34   Currently this service is only available in select areas. More information is available in the resources section.

35   More information on this website is in the resources section.

content that will help build your reputation as an expert. But remember that you can't reach your entire target audience with a class or even semester of classes and speaking engagements. And in an increasingly digital world it's possible for quality and quantity to co-exist. As an example of this consider the Khan Academy,[36] it's a high quality online school that offers free classes which are math and science based. Could you do something similar? Now is a great time to think outside of the box and think of innovative ways to engage your audience.

You know now:

    * That traditional ways of building your reputation as an expert aren't enough to reach everyone.

    * That examples exist for creating valuable extra content.

You're now considering:

    * What additional content you can offer.

    * What types of additional content will appeal to your audience and your market.

Exercise: Make a list of all of the potential additional content you can think of offering to build your credibility. Don't hold back. At this point nothing is too silly or outrageous. In a day come back to your list. Think about what you know about your market and your audience. Is there anything on this list that'll especially appeal to them? Is there anything that would outright offend them? How much of this is actually feasible for you to do?

---

36   Check out www.khanacademy.org.

Try this: Visit the website http://www.pixton.com/.[37] It's a free site that allows you to create online comics. Use it to get your creativity flowing or if you think it'll appeal to your audience create a comic specifically for them.

Try this: Check out http://www.roku.com/developer.[38] This site offers information on creating a channel specifically for the Roku.[39] This could be an interesting way to reach a much broader audience than you ever imagined and in a more innovative way than you may have thought of before.

Maintaining your credibility

In order to maintain your credibility there are two things that you'll always need to keep in mind. The first is that there's a difference between selling your services and sharing your knowledge. The second is that consistency in presentation is key. Ignoring either of these factors could be detrimental.

<u>Selling versus Sharing</u>

As I'm sure you're aware selling and sharing aren't the same thing. And the definitions shouldn't blur just because what you happen to be sharing is related to your practice. Sales pitches are fine but they have their place and that place is not at the end of an article, hidden in a book, during a speaking engagement, at the end of a class or hidden somewhere in your content. It's okay and recommended that you have business cards

---

37   More information on this website is available in the resources section.

38   More information on this website is available in the resources section.

39   The Roku is a streaming player that allows users to access both free and paid channels including well known options such as Netflix.

on hand but everything you do shouldn't serve as a hidden commercial for your practice. Think about it this way - you don't want everything you read, listen to or watch to be an advertisement in disguise so don't subject your audience to that kind of treatment either.

Consistency

Chances are good that if you went into a store that sold umbrellas one week and the next week the same store had moved on to selling something completely different like ashtrays that you'd find another store to shop at. The same is true for people who are looking for expert advice, they want to know that the way in which they receive the information is going to be consistent. Therefore you have to consistent when you're providing information. This doesn't mean that you can't grow, adapt or adopt other strategies but there should be something about what you're doing that is immediately recognizable as unique to you.

You know now:

* That selling and sharing should remain separate.

* That you need an element of consistency.

You're now considering:

* What can you do that will be your signature. Is there a style of writing that you'll adopt as your own? Will you have a signature tie or piece of jewelry that you wear to every speaking engagement? Is there a catchphrase that would make sense to add at the end of your podcasts?

Exercise: Consider your personality. Make a list, draw a picture or brainstorm in some other way. What element of your personality can you incorporate into your expert presentations? Is it something that your audience will notice? Is it something that they will relate to?

Next: Networking

Chapter 6: Networking

"It's not what you know, it's who you know." I'm sure you've heard that statement before. But have you ever thought about how true it actually is? I'm not discounting what you know but I want you to know that who you know can be equally if not more important. You also need to consider who actually knows you. Networking is necessary not only in your lawyer marketing efforts but for your legal practice in general. While technological connections can be amazing[40], it's vital that you know how to create and cultivate a traditional network.

This chapter is separated into two parts.

The first part focuses on relationships. You need to take into consideration both your personal and professional connections. You also need to know how to make new connections.

By the end of part one you'll be able to do all of the following:

* Identify the proper way to connect the people already in your life into your network.

* Identify the proper way to connect with your peers.

* Identify the proper way to go about building your network.

* Identify ways to maintain your network.

The second part focuses on referrals. Recommendations can be the difference between a practice that's thriving and one that's surviving.

By the end of part two you'll be able to do all of the following:

---

40   And will be discussed at length in the following chapter "Making Media work: Social Media."

* Understand quality versus quantity in terms of recommendations.

* Identify which recommendations you should turn down.

* Identify ways to obtain recommendations.

What you'll need for this chapter:

* One of your current business cards.

* A pencil and a piece of paper or an empty computer file.

* An internet connection.

Relationships

I have a colleague who lives in an area where within walking distance there are literally a dozen different barber shops. On one block alone there are three, with two just a few doors away from each other and one almost directly across the street. All of these barber shops are continually packed and are visibly doing well in an area where other, more diverse businesses have failed. This isn't an anomaly. It's an example of the power of good relationships. Each barbershop performs the same basic functions. And each has cultivated a loyalty within its clients so that the shops are able to co-exist without conflict. Do you have the same relationship with your clients? Do you have the same relationship with your direct competition?

<u>Developing relationships - personal</u>

Think fast: how many people do you personally know who can use your legal services in the next year? Now consider how many of those people may actually come to you for those services. Chances are good that the numbers are different, perhaps drastically so. This isn't necessarily a reflection of your skill as a lawyer. But it could serve as a reflection on your relationship building skills.

In the last chapter we discussed the importance of selling versus sharing. The same way it's important that you share your information as opposed to attempting to always sell it as a matter of maintaining your credibility as an expert, it's important that in networking situations you have the same attitude in mind. Networking is not working in the sense that you need to look at everyone in terms of potential monetary gain. Consider that there are people, even people in your market, who don't need your services and that it isn't always appropriate to make a sales pitch.

However, on the flip side you should look at all working as a chance at networking. There are a number of ways that this can be done:

* Even when you're not selling your services you are selling yourself.

Remember that you're always a representation of your practice. One way to build personal relationships is to realize that your behavior acts as a reflection of your work. You want people to respect your practice and so you need to carry yourself in a manner that makes respecting you easy.

* Make yourself memorable.

A few chapters back we talked about the importance of branding. A big part of treating your practice as a brand is to ensure that you create marketing materials which aren't only distinctly your own but also memorable. However you need to be memorable as well. And the memory you conjure needs to be a good one. Don't be afraid to set a routine and make yourself a regular at a local coffee shop or restaurant. This is a good way to get to know the people who work in your area and to strike up natural conversations about what you do for a living. If you always have a smile or a kind word as well people are more likely to think of you first when they need legal help.

* Don't continuously offer discounts.

There's nothing wrong with doing a pro bono case or even doing a few of these cases on a regular basis if both your schedule and bank account can handle it. But you don't want to get in the habit of offering discounted services in the hopes that they'll generate more business. This is a practice that without a doubt will backfire in one of two ways. You'll either be thought of as a cheap alternative to a "real" lawyer or people will always expect that your services are low price. While you may get a lot of clients this way, and those clients may recommend their friends you have to ask yourself if this is really the client base you want to build and the network you want to have?

* Don't badmouth the competition.

Being negative is never a good way to work towards building relationships. The only thing you'll gain by talking badly about your competitors is a reputation that you won't want. Remember that no one wants to feel judged, especially not someone looking for legal help. So hold your tongue and refrain from saying nasty things about other people, especially other lawyers. You may, of course, have an occasional slip but don't make it a habit.

You know now:

  * That not everyone in your market will need your legal services.

  * That even when you're not selling your services, you're selling yourself.

  * That you need to be memorable in a good way.

  * That discounted services may build your network in the short run but are problematic in the long run.

  * That you shouldn't speak badly about your competition.

You're now considering:

  * Ways to positively present yourself.

Exercise: Look critically at your business card. Consider if you were given the card, is it something you would keep? Is it something you'd toss out? What do you think people are ultimately doing with your card? Why? If necessary how could you improve it to be a better reflection of your practice.

<u>Developing relationships - professional</u>

  Building relationships with your peers is as important as building relationships with potential clients. There are two ways in which this is done. The first is via traditional relationship building. The second is via digital relationship building.

  * Traditional relationship building.

Traditional relationship building focuses on doing things the way that they were done before the internet. That means going to local mixers for professionals, attending alumni events and attending conventions that are relevant to your field even if they're not strictly for lawyers.

* Digital relationship building.

Digital relationship building focuses on utilizing the internet to connect with your peers. You may immediately be thinking of social networking but that is not the only means of peer-to-peer communication or connection. Consider all of the following sites and resources, which the internet offers for professional individuals looking to connect.

http://www.linkedin.com/ If you don't already have a profile on this website take some time to set one up. The current network is over 100 million users so it's a good place to establish and solidify connections. Consider that in addition to being able to post what you're currently doing and what jobs that you have done that you're also able to post and look for jobs as well as post and look for past classmates and colleagues.

http://www.branchout.com. This is the largest professional networking service on Facebook. It allows for users to find jobs, get leads, seek out talent and build better working relationships. Currently it is only available to Facebook users.

http://www.meetup.com. This site allows for users to meet online in order to plan offline events in their local areas. You can either join an existing meet-up group or begin one of your own.

You know now:

* That you need to look for various ways to develop relationships with your peers.

* That social networks are not the only digital platform for making connections.

You're now considering:

* Ways to make the most of the traditional and digital relationship building opportunities that are available to you.

Exercise: Spend some time exploring both the traditional and digital ways that you can connect with your peers. Look at your schedule and pick two events to attend. Additionally give yourself a goal to obtain the contact information of at least three of your peers from each event.

Maintaining relationships

If you're going to take the time to develop relationships, you also need to be prepared to take the time to maintain those relationships. What you'll need to do in order to accomplish this will vary from person to person, but it's important that you do your part to keep a connection alive. Here are some tips that may help.

* Remember important dates.

One way to keep in touch with connections is to remember the important dates that they've shared with you and to acknowledge that in some way. This can be as simple as sending a holiday e-card for major holidays such as Christmas or Hanukkah or made more personal by sending a birthday e-card. Stick to designs that are fairly generic and sentiments that aren't overly familiar as you still want to present a professional demeanor.

* Share your major news.

Are you releasing your first book? Did you book a major speaking engagement? News like this can serve as a good reason to send a brief email to your contacts.

* Share some of your professional finds.

Sometimes when we come across something that we feel will give us an edge in business rather than sharing the information, we hoard it. There are times though when this isn't a good idea. If you find something that may help one of your peers it can be beneficial for you to share it. A good example of this is if you attend a regular mixer that you know someone else could gain some insight from attending as well. By extending a casual invite you show that you're secure in your own practice.

You know now:

* That without plans to maintain your relationships that there's no point in building them.

You're now considering:

* Ways in which you can keep in contact that's unobtrusive and informative.

Try this: Go to http://www.hallmark.com/online/ and sign up. This site will allow you to add and update an address book to make e-card sending easier for important dates.

Referrals

One of the clearest signs of a job well done is that someone is willing to recommend you to someone else. However, you need to understand that all referrals aren't equal, there are some recommendations you don't want at all and that there's no secret formula to obtaining great referrals.

<u>Quality versus quantity</u>

If you had the choice would you rather have five pairs of custom made jeans that were tailored to fit you perfectly or fifty pairs of off-the-rack jeans in various sizes with some that only sort of fit you, some that didn't fit at all and one or two that you looked okay in? Most people would take the first option, preferring the guarantee of pieces that fit well versus the uncertainty of the other option. You need to apply similar logic when accepting recommendations and referrals; you want to be sure that it's the right fit for you and your practice. Ultimately you may end up accepting fewer referrals but in doing so you can be content in the knowledge that the ones you do accept are actually going to benefit you.

<u>Be Selective</u>

Not all referrals are good referrals and so you need to be prepared to be selective. You may wish to turn down a recommendation for whatever reason, here are some situations where that should absolutely be the case:

* Referrals that you don't have time for.

There are only 24 hours in the day and you can't spend all of them practicing law. There are going to be times when you want to say yes to something or someone but it'd be better if you said no. It's a better business practice to turn down something you want to do but can't than it is to accept it and not be able to give it as much attention as it truly deserves.

* Referrals that you don't want to accept.

You don't have to say yes to every client or every project that comes your way. While working for someone else you may have to do this more often than you like but when you have your own practice you shouldn't continue the habit. It's better that you have a handful of clients that you're willingly representing as opposed to dozens of clients that you don't really want.

* Referrals that could cause a conflict of interest.

Don't ever knowingly do anything that could call your ethics or the ethics of your practice into question. If you're unsure if a case or client will create a conflict of interest, don't accept it.

* Referrals that fall outside of your area of expertise.

Sometimes people forget that lawyers don't know everything about the law. And so, while it may be well-intentioned, they make recommendations that don't really fit into our areas of expertise. If one of these referrals comes your way, just politely let the person know it isn't your exact field and if possible pass them on to someone who can help.

Getting referrals

There are two guaranteed ways for you to get referrals. One, do great work. And two, give good recommendations for others when you can.

The first may seem like a no-brainer but you may end up surprising yourself at just how good you can be when you decide that you're going to treat every client as if they're your only client and every competitor as if they're no threat at all. When you focus on making your practice the best it can be people will take positive notice of that and share their experience with others.

The second is simply a matter of treating people how you want to be treated. When someone provides you with good service don't just let them know, let other people know as well. Not everyone will reciprocate this, but there will definitely be those who do.

You know now:

* That a few fitting referrals are better than tons of referrals that don't benefit you.

* That you should be selective about the referrals that you accept.

* That doing great work is a good way to get referrals.

* That referring other people is a good way to get referrals.

You're now considering:

* Ways in which you can gain more quality referrals.

Try this: Go to https://www.referralkey.com/.[41] This website helps you build and maintain a network of reciprocal referrals.

Next: Making Media Work: Social Media

---

41   More information on the website is available in the resources section.

Chapter 7: Making Media Work: Social Media

Social media is defined as forms of electronic communication where users create online communities to share information, ideas and personal content.[42] The key word in that definition is 'personal', that's because social media is about expressing your personality and interacting with your market in a way that let's them learn more about your practice. They're invited to learn about you as well, at least to the extent that you're willing to share that information. Being open to using social media is necessary for moving forward, and there are many options available.

This chapter is separated into two parts.

The first part focuses on social networks. There's a good chance that you already belong to at least one of these on a personal level. It's necessary to know how to navigate them from a professional standpoint.

By the end of part one you'll be able to do all of the following:

* Identify the do's and don'ts of Facebook profiles.

* Know how to optimize your Twitter usage.

* Identify which type of social network is best for your practice.

The second part of this chapter focuses on social sharing sites and the ways that they can work for your practice. This may not be a marketing strategy that you initially considered but it could prove very helpful.

By the end of part two you'll be able to do all of the following:

---

42   Definition courtesy of http://www.merriam-webster.com/dictionary/social%20media.

* Identify different types of social sharing sites.

* Choose which social sharing sites would be best for you to utilize.

What you'll need for this chapter:

* A pencil and a piece of paper or an empty computer file.

* An internet connection.

Social networks

If you belong to Facebook or Twitter you're already a member of a social network. The question is whether you're using it in a way that's beneficial for your marketing. If you don't belong to these social networks, you should look into joining immediately.

Facebook

Before considering anything else, you need to make sure that your basic profile information is properly setup. This includes not only making sure that the information is up to date but also that it's the best possible reflection of your practice. I strongly suggest that when utilizing Facebook you set up two profiles, one for yourself and one for your practice.[43] These profiles may have some of the same characteristics.

Personal Profiles

When I use the term personal profile I'm not referring to a profile that almost no one but close friends see. Instead I'm referring to a profile that's for you as opposed to for your law firm or practice. However this

---

43   This may or may not be possible if you're working at a law firm, check with any rules and regulations that they have regarding the usage of social networks.

profile still needs to have your professional image in mind which means there are some definite things you should include and some definite things that you should avoid.

Do include at least one clear picture of yourself. This can be a professional image or any crisp, recent image. You can, and should also include any images that you may have which show you engaged in activities related to your practice like speaking at a conference or receiving an award.

Don't include images that people may find juvenile or offensive or pictures that make it seem as if you're untrustworthy or don't take your job seriously. Also if a friend tags you in a shot that fits this criteria, immediately untag yourself.

Do list the college and law school you attended. Also be sure to include any foreign languages that you speak fluently.

Don't make light of education by listing things like "School of hard knocks" on your profile. Similarly don't list languages like Pig-Latin, Klingon on Gibberish. Your friends may relate to that or find it funny but clients won't respect it.

Do list your current city and state. You want people to have a general idea of where you're located. Be sure to update this if you move.

Don't include information such as your cell phone number.

Do make sure to post on a regular basis. Later in the chapter there will be more in depth information on what to post.

Don't let your page get cluttered with things like game apps. While you want people to know that you're an active member of the community you don't want them attempting to friend you only because they need another neighbor in Farmville.

Professional Profiles

This is the profile that will represent your practice. It needs to be clear and easy to navigate. You'll need to follow all of do's and dont's of a personal profile but you should also include all of the following:

* Your website information.

* Your office hours and location.

* Any relevant links.[44]

You'll also want to be sure to avoid making negative comments about your competitors, judges or your clients. The "problem" with social network status updates is that they allow us to post instantly without necessarily thinking the consequences through. Don't fall into this trap.

When utilizing a social network there are only three things that you need to be doing. You need to be informing, offering invitations and providing interaction.

Informing

In the past couple of chapters we've discussed the importance of sharing as opposed to selling when you're marketing. This is especially true when it comes to the postings that you place on social networks. You want to let those viewing your page know that you're knowledgeable about your professed area of expertise but you don't want every status

---

[44] This includes links to information that establishes you as an expert i.e. where your books can be purchased or when your next speaking engagement is if it's open to the public.

update to read like copy for a promo piece. Here are some examples of status updates that inform:

1) Asset protection is like insurance, you buy it with the hopes that you won't need it-but if you do need it, its there. #assets #presser[45]

This post is geared towards people who know what asset protection is as well as those who don't. For someone who knows what asset protection is, they can recognize how true that statement is. And it may make them look at their own lives and realize that they need more protection than they currently have. For someone who doesn't know what asset protection is, this compares it to something that's familiar to everyone, giving them an idea of how it may work. The goal is for that person to ask questions. Additionally by adding hashtags[46] you can immediately copy and paste the posting into Twitter.[47]

2) How bad is the litigation problem in America? View our Blog for the answer. #assets #presser

http://www.assetprotectionattorneys.com/Asset_Protection_Blog/2012/ February/How_bad_is_the_litigation_problem_in_America_.aspx

Yes, this post can be considered as a promotion. But at the same time it also provides information that's relevant to my practice as well as being of interest to my market. Feel free to link to your blog or website in your

---

45   All of the examples being used are actual status updates from my personal Facebook page https://www.facebook.com/hillelpresser.

46   Hashtags are the # symbol. By placing them in front of specific words it allows those terms to be searched for so that you can see every posting that has that specific tag. While this is used on Twitter as that's what it was created for there are Facebook postings that will include them as well.

47   Remember that Twitter has a character limit though so this won't work for longer posts.

post just make sure that it's done with a clear purpose and that you deliver on the promise you make.

Inviting

Status updates which are inviting in nature can come in one of three formats.

1) These types of updates can invite viewers to go and check out information on an external site, similar to the second status update above.

2) These types of updates can be actual invitations inviting people to events such as book signings.[48]

3) These types of updates can invite people to give you information. This can be a tricky option. Remember that you're presenting yourself as both a lawyer and an expert so don't ask questions which you should know the answer to in a public forum. Instead ask for suggestions on things such as a quiet place to have lunch in your area. Such postings allow the best option for interacting with the people viewing your page.

Interact

Interactions are a key part of being a member of a social network. If someone responds to one of your status updates then be sure to acknowledge it. Even one or two words can be sufficient. Additionally if someone posts a comment on your page, be sure to respond to it. This is especially important if the comment is a negative one. Just remember to be professional and courteous, and to be sure to follow through on any promises you may make. For example, if you offer to call someone to

---

48   In going this route be sure that you have actual individual invitations as well which can be sent via email or regular mail.

settle a situation privately or if you agree to attend a function, make sure that you do so.

You know now:

    * That ideally you will have both a personal and professional Facebook page.

    * That your pages need to be free of apps and other games that may take away from your professional image.

    * That you should have at least one clear and recent image.

    * That you should include pertinent information such as where you went to law school and your current city.

    * That status updates are meant to be inviting or informing.

    * That you should interact with people who comment on your updates or post on your page.

You're now considering:

    * What you need to remove from your Facebook page(s).

    * What you can add to your Facebook page(s).

Try this: Go to https://lujure.com.[49] This is a site that will allow you to build a customized front page for your professional profile. There are drag and drop options which make it easy to use and plans range from free to $300 per month.

---

49   More information on this site is available in the resources section.

Twitter

Twitter bills itself as a real-time information network[50] and that's a fair assessment. Tweets are concise and can be posted by any member at any time. It may seem that in such a landscape that you couldn't possibly standout but there are three things that may help. The first is the type of content you're posting. The second is the strategic usage of hashtags and the third is when you're tweeting.

Content type

Each tweet is limited to 140 characters. This forces you to be word economic. And that word economy can work as an advantage. Just remember that as with Facebook status updates your Tweets should be informative or inviting and that whenever possible you should interact with others.

Hashtags

When you're utilizing Twitter for your marketing, hashtags aren't an option. Using them will allow your tweets to be searched by people looking for those exact terms and words. If you're at a loss regarding what hashtags to use here are some tips to keep in mind:

* Use a hashtag that relates to your specialty. I'm an asset protection lawyer so I use #assets in all of my posts. Similarly if you're a patent lawyer you may want to try #patent or #inventor.

* Check out which hashtags are being used in real time. One way to so this is by going to http://trendsmap.com/.[51] One of the best

---

50   https://twitter.com/about.

51   More information on this site is available in the resources section.

features of this site is that the topics which are being trended situate over a map of the United States so you can see both what people are talking about most and get a general idea of where they're located. This can help you to hone in on what people in your area are trending.

* Make sure your hashtags are relevant. This may seem like a no-brainer but it's better for you to include one or two hashtags that make sense than taking on three or four that may or may not work.

When should you tweet

Once you begin tweeting you want to make sure that you do so on a regular basis. You may feel as if you don't have the time to commit to keeping both Facebook and Twitter up-to-date but there are some things you can do to ensure that both are being utilized:

* Post the same things on both Twitter and Facebook. While there will be people who follow you on both sites, there will also be those who choose to only follow you on one. By posting the same message on both sites you're ensuring that everyone is getting the same message.

* Schedule a time to tweet. You can either do this by making time once a week to do so on your own or you can use an online service that will auto-schedule your tweets. One site to try is Timely[52] they analyze your last 199 tweets and determine the times which your tweets will have the most impact.

After having figured out what to tweet and when to tweet the question is who are you tweeting to. Your twitter posts don't mean a thing if you don't have followers who are reading them who can appreciate or

---

52   http://timely.is/#/.

use their content and who as a result may use your services. There are a number of individuals and even companies that offer to sell you Twitter followers. I don't suggest that you go that route as there's no way of knowing where these people are from or if they are even actual people as opposed to robots. While you want your tweets seen, you want them seen by people who are interested specifically in what you have to say, not people who had the misfortune of being on the wrong mailing list.

Here are some tips on gaining followers:

* Tell the people you know that you use Twitter. Again this may seem like a no-brainer but you'd be amazed by how many people don't think of this initially.

* Add your Twitter information to places where it's pertinent. Add a "follow me" button on your website or blog and depending on your market, add it to your business card as well. Also be sure to include it with the information on your Facebook profile.

* Make sure that you follow people. And let them know that you're doing so. A good way to do this is by using the follow Friday hashtag[53] which allows you to suggest other Twitter users to follow. This could be an especially powerful tool if you work at a law firm and everyone uses your Twitter feeds to promote each other.

* Offer incentives to people who follow you. For instance you could announce that you're having a tweet-up[54] where those in attendance will get a private Q&A session with you before or after a book signing or

---

53   #followfriday.

54   An offline gathering of Twitter followers.

speaking engagement. Make sure that you add this not just to your Twitter feed but also to Facebook and your website. While it will probably take some extra coordination and may require permission from whoever is holding the event, sites such as http://twtvite.com/[55] will help you to set up the tweet-up.

You know now:

> * That your tweets need to be informing and inviting.

> * That you should utilize hashtags.

> * That you can search which hashtags are trending in your area.

> * That you can schedule tweets.

> * That there are legitimate ways for you to increase followers.

You're now considering:

> * What hashtags will be relevant to the majority of your posts.

> * Whether or not you can hold a tweet-up.

Exercise: Write up or type up something that you think would make a good tweet. Look at it critically. Does it meet the requirement of being 140 characters or less? If not, what can you take out so that it still makes sense but meets the requirement. If it is the right length, is it informative? Is it inviting? What hashtags would work with it? Practice creating additional tweets as well.

---

55   More information on this site is available in the resource section.

Social sharing sites

As a lawyer you may not immediately see the advantages of utilizing a social sharing site. However, you shouldn't discount the impact that your involvement in these online communities can have in terms of reaching your market. While there are numerous social sharing sites out there, for the purpose of this book the focus is going to be on two of the larger sites, YouTube and Pinterest.

YouTube

You're probably already highly familiar with YouTube, the site's been around for quite a while and it's very popular. What you may not have considered are the ways in which it can be used to help you market. Here are some tips on the type of content that could be added to your YouTube page:[56]

* Videos that showcase you speaking, teaching or answering questions. If you can get footage from a conference or something similar that would be best. However if you can film something high quality on your own, you may want to consider doing weekly or monthly videos to post. Additionally, if you advertise on television you may want to put copies of your commercials on YouTube as well.

* Book trailers[57] for your most recent work.

---

[56]   Make sure that you have the proper permissions to include any content before you add it.

[57]   Just like movie trailers advertise upcoming movies, book trailers do the same thing for books.

* Videos that showcase any positive media that you may have received. While this can be actual news coverage, it can also be a tasteful slideshow that features newspaper clippings, etc.

Once you've decided on what you can post there are some basic do's and don'ts that you should be aware of when using YouTube for your legal marketing.

Do set up a YouTube channel[58] so that all of your videos can be found in one place.

Don't make the information on your YouTube channel hard to read. Think about color scheme and background and make sure the text is legible.

Do post varied types of videos, ones that showcase your skills and accomplishments.

Don't post content that isn't relevant. As much as something may interest you on a personal level, don't add it to your YouTube channel if it isn't related to your practice.

Do comment on videos that are relevant to your practice and reply if users comment on your videos.

Don't enable comments on your videos if you don't have the time to monitor or respond to them. You don't want your page cluttered with spam or unanswered questions.

---

58   A YouTube channel is the homepage for your account, it will show the account name, type and public videos you've uploaded. It will also show the information you added. For more information on this check the resources section.

You know now:

* That you should set up a YouTube channel to reach more of your market.

* That there are a variety of things you can post on YouTube.

* That your YouTube content and comments should be relevant to your practice.

You're now considering:

* What video you currently have that can be utilized.

* Whether or not you should film or create your own videos.

Try this: www.slideroll.com.[59] This is a free service which allows users to create slideshows that can then be uploaded to YouTube. If you don't have any video currently available this could be a good way to create something for you to put onto YouTube. Try making a 30-60 second informational piece. This could be especially helpful if you have a highly specialized practice or there are a lot of misconceptions about the type of law you do.

Pinterest

Pinterest[60] is a visual bookmarking site which allows users to pin their online finds to virtual boards.[61] Your first thought may be that such a place is no place for marketing, especially lawyer marketing. You'd be

---

59   More information on this site is available in the resources section.

60   http://pinterest.com/.

61   The key word in that sentence is visual so you can only pin images and videos that the site recognizes which means sites that are all text and those with flash are usually off limits.

wrong. You choose the names of your boards and what goes on them which allows you a different way to approach marketing. Rather than saying "This is who I am" pin boards instead say "This is what I like; this is what I recommend." And provided your boards are public anyone can see your pins, like them, comment on them and even re-pin them to their own boards. When you have a website, blog, YouTube channel, etc. Some basic do's and don'ts are as follows:

Do choose the name of your board wisely. You want something that people are likely to recognize. For example, if you're a corporate attorney you may choose a name like "Business Law Basics."

Don't use your name as the name of your board, or the name of your law firm, for one it's too blatantly an advertisement and two unless your incredibly famous chances are good no one will have any idea about what the board is about.

Do use some of your own content. Include your website, a few relevant blog posts or a link to your podcasts and/or YouTube channel.

Don't pin your content exclusively. Mix it up with other relevant content you find online. For example, if you're a lawyer who handles international adoptions you may include a pin that links to the website of an author that wrote a really great book on the subject. Or if you're a prosecutor you may want to include a pin that links to the site for an anonymous tip line in your area or a victim support group.

Do take the time to describe your pins so that other users know where they lead.

Don't make your descriptions vague or misleading. Also be sure that you're not using language that's based on trying to sell someone on your practice.

Do follow other users and boards.

Don't get discouraged if people aren't following you back.

You know now:

    * That you can use a visual bookmarking site as a part of your marketing.

    * That you want to vary your content so that it doesn't all lead to your website, blog etc.

You're now considering:

    * What types of boards you can create.

Exercise: Write out your specialty. Now think of all of the things that could be related to it in some way. Don't be afraid to think outside of the box. How many non-legal options are on the list? How many of these things have you seen online? How many of them would make logical accompaniments to pins about your practice?

Next: Making Media Work: Online Marketing

Chapter 8: Making Media Work: Online Marketing

In an increasingly digital world, a strong and focused online presence is crucial to any lawyer marketing efforts. You have to find a way for your name and your practice to be in a variety of places at once that's consistent but not redundant and authoritative but not boring. Prospective clients need to want to visit your site, read your content and click your links.

This chapter is separated into four parts.

The first part focuses on websites. You may already have a website for your practice, if so you'll still want to check this section out as it provides insight you may not have considered.

By the end of part one you'll be able to do all of the following:

* Identify how to select a domain name.

* Identify the importance of SEO.

* Identify how to find out what content is working.

* Identify how to drive traffic to your site.

The second part focuses on blogs. Even with a website, having a blog is a good idea as it provides a place where people looking for information can go without having to navigate through the other pages of your website.

By the end of part two you'll be able to do all of the following:

* Identify how to create successful blog postings.

* Identify how to increase readership.

The third part focuses on newsletters. Newsletters offer a great way for you to connect with people already on your mailing list.

By the end of part three you'll be able to do all of the following:

* Identify what type of content should be included in your mailing list.

* Identify how to potentially increase the number of people on your mailing list.

The fourth part focuses on Pay-Per-Click[62] ads. These ads are used in conjunction with search engine results, in order for you to have the best chance of attracting people interested in your services to your site.

By the end of part four you'll be able to do all of the following:

* Identify the difference between Pay-Per-Click "PPC" and Pay-Per-Impression "PPI" ads.

* Determine whether or not PPC ads would be good for your practice.

What you'll need for this chapter:

* A pencil and a piece of paper or an empty computer file.

* An internet connection.

Websites

A website devoted to your practice is one of the best tools that you have. It's a place where you can control all of the information being

---

62   Pay-Per-Click is shortened to PPC elsewhere in this chapter.

presented and allows you to present a comprehensive view of who you are as a lawyer and the services that you offer. However it's important to know that a bad website is in many ways worse than no website at all. So there are some definite things that you need to consider in regards to your site.

Domain name

The domain name of your website needs to do two main things. First it needs to be descriptive. There shouldn't be any question that it belongs to a lawyer or law firm. Secondly, your domain name needs to be professional. You don't want there to be any questions in the clients mind about whether or not you're serious about what you do. If possible your domain name should also be something that's fairly easy to remember as well as fairly easy to spell. Remember that not everyone who goes to your site will be entering through a link so try to avoid words or names that are difficult to pronounce and if you must utilize a longer name try something that flows well. For example my website is www.AssetProtection-Attorneys.com. It's a mouthful but it describes exactly the type of law that I do and all of the words utilized are those that are common enough that they can be spelled and shared without issue. Could it be shorter? Certainly. But other site names wouldn't have been able to convey my niche so precisely.

As an important note make sure that you're the one who purchases the domain name. This way it will belong to you even if you hire someone else to design your site. The same is true for any hosting package or plan that you purchase.

Design

Having selected a domain name or a series of potential domain names[63] you can begin to think about design. It should go without saying but you want a site that has a clean look and is easy to read and navigate. Beyond that there are two types of web design, the type that you do on your own and the type that you'll hire a person or company to do for you. Both have their pros and cons and it's important that they're explored.

If you build your own site chances are good that unless you have a graphic design and coding background that you're going to be using a WYSIWYG editor.[64] The primary pro of this is the fact that you're the one in control of the entire process, you know what's going up and when it's going up. Additionally, these sites are fairly easy to set up and you could have a site online in a few days or even a few hours.

However, if you go this route it's important to note that there will be some definite limitations in place. The first is that you'll need to use a template and that this template will only allow for minor modifications if it allows for any modifications at all. Secondly, there may be serious restrictions regarding the amount of traffic you can have each month, whether or not you can utilize contact forms and if there are any issues with the site or template you more than likely will not simply be able to make a call in order to rectify the issue.

If you decide to hire a professional to build your site the burdens of design and implementation fall to someone else. The pros of this are

---

63   It's highly suggested that you do the latter, you'd be amazed by how many domain names are already taken.

64   WYSIWYG stands for "what you see is what you get" these editors allow you to work without knowledge of html.

that it frees your time to do something else related to your practice. Also it'll be possible for you to get a custom site, in the exact color scheme that you want.

There are also cons of outsourcing the building of your site. You have to rely on someone else to do all the work and that work can be delayed or halted right when you need it to be moving forward. Also you need to find someone that you work well with as this will more than likely be a relationship that goes on for at least a few weeks. Don't be afraid to look around to find a web designer or web design firm that feels like the best possible fit for you.

Whether you design the site yourself, or hire someone else to do it, realize that you may have to be flexible regarding the design. Just because you can envision something in your head doesn't mean that you'll be good at explaining it well enough for it to be executed. Additionally certain layouts, color choices or font selections simply won't work together. Be prepared to alter what you may immediately have in mind.

SEO

SEO stands for search engine optimization, this is how well your site is recognized by the various search engines. I suggest either hiring a web designer who knows how to do this or if you build your own site hiring someone who specializes in this. Good SEO can be the difference between your site ranking near the top of search engine results and being buried twenty or thirty pages in. Here are some important things to keep in mind:

* There is no way to buy your way to the top of the search engine rankings. Anyone promising to place you on the first page of Google or any other search engine is attempting to scam you.

* Flash websites aren't SEO friendly.[65] This isn't to say that all flash websites don't have their place, they do. But generally they aren't recommended for small brands or local companies.

* You need to think about keywords. While a massive vocabulary is a great thing, when writing content for your website keep your language simple as this increases the chances that what's on your site will match a word or phrase that's being search for.

Content

Your website will likely contain a few basic pages including a home page, an about us, a list of your services offered and a contact page. Beyond that, what you add will truly be up to you and what you feel your market will respond to. My suggestion is that you include links to related and relevant resources as well as valuable free content[66] in addition to the basic pages.

It's important to note that there are ways of determining what your website visitors are looking at and what they're ignoring. Sites such as Google analytics[67] and it's add-on footprint live[68] are free services that

---

65   http://www.seo.com/blog/merging-flash-seo/.

66   Valuable free content is content that users aren't likely to get elsewhere such as a personal consultation if you can handle the commitment they entail.

67   http://www.google.com/analytics/. More information on this site is available in the resources section.

68   http://footprintlive.com/. More information on this site is available in the resources section.

let you track trends related to your content. This information may help you make decisions regarding whether or not additional content should be added in the future or if there's content that you currently have that needs to be reworked or removed.

Traffic

Getting traffic on your website can be problematic, especially when your site is new. Aside from adding your site address to your business cards and social media pages, you may not feel as if there's much that you can do to legitimately boost hits. One suggestion is to utilize a service such as cloudflood[69] which drives traffic to your site via Facebook posts and Tweets. These messages aren't spam. Instead they're posted by real people who do so in order to receive exclusive content from you. While such a service will require you to create content to be used as a loss leader it can serve as a means of getting you additional traffic from people who are interested in your services.

You know now:

    * That your domain name should be descriptive, fairly easy to spell and easy to remember.

    * That you should purchase your domain.

    * That your site design should be clean and easy to navigate.

    * The pros and cons of building your own site.

    * The pros and cons of hiring a web designer.

    * That you can't buy a high search engine rank.

* That flash sites aren't SEO friendly.

* That your site language should be simple.

* That there are ways to track which of your web pages are drawing the most traffic.

* That it's possible to legitimately draw traffic to your site by using a loss leader.

You're now considering:

* Multiple domain names.

* What you can utilize as a loss leader in order to draw traffic to your site.

Exercise: Write out your specialty. How can that be translated into a domain name? How many different domain names can you come up with? Are they easy to spell? Are they easy to remember? Do the words that make up the name flow well together?

Try this: Go to http://www.scorpiondesign.com/ a web design firm that focuses on lawyer websites. Their own website serves as a prime example of many of the components that they can add into a site in order to make it both dynamic and unique. Additionally, they offer complete customization and offer constant and consistent support. Ask for Peter C. Webb at (866) 332-3230 and he will help get you set up with your very own lawyer website!

---

69   http://cloudflood.com/. More information on this site is available in the resources section.

Blogs

Blogs are a great way to create a near constant stream of content for you to share with your market. They offer an outlet for you to share your expertise and can be an easy way to reach a wide audience.

How to write a successful blog post

There's no secret formula to a successful blog. There are however two key things which you need to keep in mind, including the quality of your writing and the frequency of your postings. The following tips will help you in both areas.

* Make sure that your content is engaging. Tabloids are a perfect example. I am certain that you have looked at tabloids while standing in line at a store at some point in your life, whether or not you have actually purchased the magazine. The headlines grab your attention, even if only momentarily. Think of that while you're writing your blog postings. Factual doesn't have to equal boring and your blog is a good place to share your personality while also sharing insight.

* Make sure that your content is accurate. This is especially true if you're using a news story in order to illustrate a point. Be sure to double-check any facts or statistics that you are using as well.

* Avoid using an abundance of legal jargon. Yes, you want readers to know that you know what you're talking about but you also want them to be able to understand you without a dictionary. While certain terms such as "litigious" have entered into common parlance, there are others that won't be as easily recognized.

* Offer an opinion. Remember that readers can get facts from other sources, what will help to draw them to you is your interpretation of those facts. Just be sure that somewhere in the posting you also offer information on the divergent opinion as well.

* Make sure that you proofread. Check the blog for grammatical or spelling errors before you upload it.

* Post on a regular basis. Set aside time at least once a week to post to your blog.

How to increase readership

Having taken the time to create content you want to be sure that it's being read and that ideally it's being read by people who will become future clients. There are some steps that you can take towards increasing the number of people who read your blog:

* Do interviews and ask for readers to suggest questions. Interviews allow readers a different level of insight than narrative stories provide. And when you add an element of interaction you increase the likelihood that readers will return to see if their questions where among the ones that were utilized.

* Offer to do guest blog postings. If you have colleagues with blogs you can offer to do a guest post on their blog in exchange for them doing the same on your blog. The benefit of this is that it can potentially increase readers for both blogs. Additionally, if you have a hobby and follow a blog on the subject there's no harm in contacting the author of that blog and offering your services as a guest blogger. In both instances

your blog address will be available for readers who may not have already seen your blog.

* Try a blog carnival.[70] A blog carnival is a collection of blog posts all by different authors centered around a single topic. The benefit of this is that while readers will have a variety of postings to read that they're interested in the specific topic which they're searching for which more than likely means that they're interested in the information that you have to offer.

You know now:

* That your blog posts should be engaging.

* That your blog should be accurate.

* That you should avoid using legal jargon which readers may not understand.

* That you should express your opinion.

* That it's important to proofread.

* That your blog should have scheduled posting updates.

* That readership can be improved by doing interviews.

* That readership can be improved by doing guest blogging.

* That blog carnival participation can increase readership.

* That it's possible to legitimately draw traffic to your site by using a loss leader.

You're now considering:

* Multiple domain names.

* What you can utilize as a loss leader in order to draw traffic to your site.

Try this: http://www.freeconferencecall.com/[71] allows you to do interviews over the phone and save the audio, this can then be added to your blog.

Newsletters

Newsletters are a proven way for individuals and companies to connect with people who've opted in to receiving information about their services. Additionally, newsletters require less of a time commitment than blogs do as they're generally only available once a month. As a lawyer you may not immediately feel as if you could utilize a newsletter to your advantage. But you can. You just need to be sure that you have the right type of content and that you're capable of reaching as many people as possible.

Content

You certainly can't share details of your cases so it may be confusing trying to think about what you can write about once a month that your newsletter readers may not have already seen somewhere else. Here are some suggestions on what to include mix and match until you find a formula that works for you and your practice:

---

70   http://blogcarnival.com/bc/index.php More information on this site is available in the resources section.

71   More information on this site is available in the resources section.

* A calendar of events for the month. This is an especially important edition if you have a lot of events which are open to the public. Be sure to also include any RSVP and location information.

* A recap of your blog postings for the month. Briefly summarize the blog posts that you have written and leave out enough information that readers are enticed, increasing the likelihood that they'll view your blog.

* An op-ed piece on a current event that's relevant to your practice. Don't offer legal advice. Instead, summarize the case and offer your opinion on something general like the potential effect it could have on your field overall.

* Spotlight a local business in your area and see if they'll offer a coupon to readers. Since the business is being highlighted they'll be more likely to carry a copy of your physical newsletter or place a link to your digital copy on their website.

Once you've thought about content consider a means of distribution. Traditionally newsletters have been available in paper format. But this can create a lot of waste. Additionally, it may limit options regarding the usage of images, etc. However, if this is the format that your market is most likely to respond to and you think that they may be reluctant to embrace change then by all means go this route.

For a more updated way to distribute content, think about making it email friendly. An emailed newsletter lets you know exactly who's receiving it. Just be sure that you have permission to send it to the email addresses that you have on your email list.

<u>Growing your mailing list</u>

It may be tempting to do so but you don't want to buy a mailing list. Similar to purchasing Twitter followers, oftentimes the people on these lists haven't expressed any interest in your content[72] and just have the bad luck of having their email addresses sold. Instead you want to grow your list organically. There are a few ways to do that:

* Ask people to sign up for your newsletter. Inform them that their email address will never be shared or sold and let them know that they can unsubscribe at any time. Be sure to make the sign up process simple and include links on your web page, blog and social media sites.

* Make sure that your newsletter is easy to find. People are more likely to sign up for something when they know precisely where it is.

* Offer a sample of your newsletter. This lets potential readers know upfront what to expect and will help them to make a more informed decision regarding whether or not they want to sign up.

You know now:

* That newsletters are a good way to reach out to clients.

* That there is no strict format your newsletter needs to follow.

* That your newsletter can be in either paper or electronic format

* That you should only send your newsletter to people you have permission to send it to.

* That an easy to find newsletter may help increase readers.

* That a sample letter may help increase readers.

You're now considering:

> *What you could include in your own newsletter.

Exercise: If you were creating a newsletter what content would you want to include in it? Do you think that the content you've selected will resonate with your market?

Try this: Go to http://simplebooklet.com/.[73] This site allows users to design their own booklets. These are full color and can support images and text. They can be used in place of traditional newsletters and have additional reach as they can be used on blogs, websites and social media sites.

PPC Ads

PPC ads are ads that are placed according to search engine results. Additionally they can appear on selected websites which have related content.

PPC Basics

For many people this is the most cost effective method of advertising as the budget is set up at the beginning of the month and in many instances, such as with Google adwords,[74] you only pay when your ads are clicked. There are numerous companies which offer these services so there is no true standard but here are some general tips that will help you chose the service that is best for you:

---

72   Which increases the likelihood that they'll opt out anyway.

73   More information on this site is available in the resources section.

74   adwords.google.com/. More information on this site is available in the resources section.

*Check whether the service they're offering is Pay-Per-Click or Pay-Per-Impression. With PPC ads, you'll pay based on the number of people that click on your ad and visit your website. With PPI ads you're paying for the number of people that see your ad. Decide if what's more important for your practice is people visiting your website or people seeing your ad where they may or may not click the link.

* Consider the cost of the keyword associated with your ad. The general rule of thumb is that the more broad or popular a term, the more costly it will be per ad. Weigh whether it's more important that your ad appears when someone types in "Lawyers" or if you can be more specific.

* Check to see if you can control the location where the ads appear. If you have a small practice and you don't travel outside of your local area you want to be sure that your ads are only being shown locally.

* See if you can ad images. Images may increase the chances of people clicking on your ad. See if they can be included and if so how much additional they cost.

Should you invest in PPC ads

Ultimately only you can decide if PPC ads are right for your practice. Consider both your market and the potential pros and cons as they relate specifically to the services that you're considering using. You may also want to try an inexpensive test run before committing to spending for money on a larger campaign if you do decide PPC ads are right for you.

You know now:

* The exact difference between PPC and PPI ads.

* That different companies offering PPC ads offer different options for customizing those ads.

* That you should do an test run of a PPC service before agreeing to a more expensive campaign.

You're now considering:

* Whether or not a PPC campaign is right for your practice

Exercise: Write out several keywords that could be used in conjunction with your practice. Are they too specific? Are they not specific enough? Are they likely to be sued by people in your market?

Next: Making Media Work: Public Relations

Chapter 9: Making Media Work: Public Relations

One of the keys to a successful legal marketing campaign is a basic public relations plan. If you are looking for a great public relations company, visit www.emsincorporated.com "EMSI" or call (800) 881-7342 and ask for Marsha Friedman. EMSI will help you with all of your PR needs from radio bookings, TV appearances to writing query letters for magazines.

It's important to know that even if you're not at the point in your career where you feel as if you can justify the cost of a publicist that you don't have to sacrifice this aspect. There are steps that you can take in order to help assure that your practice is getting the type of positive press that will benefit you.

This chapter is separated into two parts.

The first part of this chapter focuses on the type of legwork that you will have to do. It's important to realize the ways in which you'll need to reach out to the media.

By the end of part one you'll be able to do all of the following:

* Identify how to write a press release.

* Identify when a press release is necessary.

* Identify how to write a query letter.

* Identify when a query letter is necessary.

The second part of the chapter focuses on the type of outlets that you should be contacting based on the size of your firm. It's important that you're realistic about the type of practice that you have in order to best maximize the types of press that would be best suited for you.

By the end of part two you'll be able to do all of the following:

* Identify what type of practice you have.

* Identify where you should focus your public relations efforts.

What you'll need for this chapter:

* A pencil and a piece of paper or an empty computer file.

* Your calendar or daily planner.[75]

* An internet connection.

The tools you need to approach the media

Just as there is a certain way in which you reach out to potential clients there is a certain protocol related to reaching out to the media. When handling public relations you need to be prepared to follow specific formulas based on the message you want to share and who you're hoping it'll reach.

Press releases

Press releases are perhaps the most common type of writing related to public relations. They're simple one page documents designed to announce something newsworthy to a large group of people at once. While the content of the releases will change based on what exactly is

---

75   It should include any events or activities that you have going on.

going on, the format of the release will remain the same.[76] Every press release has the same basic components.

The headline

This is typed in bold and every word is capitalized. It should be catchy, brief and written without a period at the end.

The subhead or summary[77]

This is a brief summary of the press release. Ideally it shouldn't be longer than one or two sentences. This shouldn't simply be a rewording of the headline, it needs to be something that stands on its own as a part of the release.

The lead paragraph

The first paragraph is started with the city, state and full date[78] followed by a dash before leading into the story. This paragraph[79] should make readers want to read more.

The body paragraphs

Additional paragraphs should cover the basic information and offer brief insight into the overall story. Use the following as prompts:

* Who is this story about?

* What is occurring?

---

76   There are numerous sites that offer press release templates for free.

77   This is optional but it may be required for certain press release distribution channels.

78   For example Boca Raton, Florida, February 15, 2012.

79   While a standard paragraph is five sentences in a press release a paragraph can be as few as three sentences.

* When is it occurring?

* Where is it occurring?

* Why is this newsworthy?

* How can the public be involved?

The final paragraph

If possible, start the final paragraph with a quote from someone other than yourself. For example, if you've written a book the quote can be from an early reviewer or the author of the foreword. Beyond that, the final paragraph should be sure to offer a final summary of anything especially important.

Boilerplate

The boilerplate is basic information about you and your practice. It shouldn't be longer than a paragraph so you'll need to find a way to be both brief and descriptive. This same information can be used in any press release that you send out. However be sure to update it, if within it you include information such as how long you've been practicing as that will obviously change.

Contact information

In list form be sure to include the name of the media contact[80], the title of the media contact[81], the full company name, the contact phone number, the contact email address and your website address.

###

---

80   If you're the media contact list your own name.
81   If you're the media contact list your own title.

Every press release is ended with three numerical symbols centered on the bottom of the page.

Here are some important things to remember when writing your own press release:

* This isn't an advertisement; it's a news story. That means that whatever you're announcing should be something that people will be interested in. Good press release topics include the opening of a new office, the release of a book or an expansion of your firm. This needs to be real news so treat it that way.

* Honesty counts. Don't try and disguise a marketing piece as a press release. If you don't have something to share that will serve as news to your market then don't try and create something. It'll ultimately only threaten your credibility.

* Make sure your information is recent. The same way in which you don't want to hear news weeks after its already happened your press release should focus on something which hasn't happened, yet but which will be happening in the near future. This allows people time to see the story.

* Be sure to proofread. Make sure that your spelling and grammar are correct. Also, any contact information for your business should be correct and up to date.

You know now:

* That all press releases follow the same format.

* That your press release should contain a real news story.

* That your press release should be honest.

* That the information in your press release shouldn't be about something that already occurred.

* That you should be sure to proofread your press release before submitting it.

* That the same bolierplate can be used on every press release that you send out.

You're now considering:

* If you have anything newsworthy that would make a good press release.

Exercise: Review your calendar. Do you have anything occurring in the next couple of weeks that could be considered news? If so, do you have ample time to write a press release[82]? If not, is there anything you can do that would provide you with a positive news story?

Try this: Go to http://www.prweb.com/[83] and set up an account. Even if you don't have anything to write a press release about right now I suggest familiarizing yourself with the site and seeing how it works.

Query letters and pitch letters

Query letters and pitch letters are essentially the same thing; they both serve as a brief introduction to you and the story that you have available. These letters should be a maximum of one page[84] and should entice the reader to want to know more. In that regard, it's important to

---

82   The event or activity should be more than 2 days in advance as many press release distribution channels will require time to review your release before making it live.

83   More information on this site is available in the resources section.

84   Unless something longer is specifically requested.

be descriptive but to avoid giving away every single detail. Here are some tips for creating your own letter:

* Use standard business letter format and make sure that you have the name of the person that you're addressing not just their title.[85]

* Make sure that the first line offers a good lead in. Remember that these are busy people reading your letters, give them a good reason to keep reading.

* Offer insight into why your particular idea will be relevant by the time they need it for their magazine, television show or radio show. Keep in mind that most story ideas are pitched months in advance so your idea needs to be something that will be topical.

* Be persuasive but not pushy. You want to offer any reasons that you have regarding why the story you're looking to share is compelling, but don't force the issue.

* Be sure to provide detailed contact information. Make sure that you supply multiple ways to be reached and if you have a preference of how contact is made be sure to state it. Also, be sure to list what times are best to make phone contact.

These letters are useful in a variety of situations. They should be your go-to pieces whenever you need to contact a radio show, a television show or a magazine. And unless the outlet specifically requests something else, like an image, then your letter should be sent by itself.

---

85   If you're emailing your pitch make sure that it's going to a direct email address and that you address the person by name rather than "To whom it may concern."

You know now:

* That the terms query letter and pitch letter are used interchangeably.

* That your letter shouldn't be longer than one page.

* That you need to address your letter to a specific person and include their title.

* That you need to be compelling from the first line.

* That your information should be relevant for when it'll actually be used.

* That you need to be persuasive.

* That your letter should have your full contact information included.

You're now considering:

* If you have anything that would make a good pitch to a radio show, television show or magazine.

Exercise: Review your calendar. Are you participating in anything in the next few months that would help coordinators consider you a good guest on their program? If so, write a sample query letter. Does it fulfill all of the requirements outlined above? Could it use some work?

The outlets that you should be approaching

It's important moving forward with your public relations campaign that you take into account two key factors, including the size of your practice and the amount of time that you have to dedicate to this particular effort. You should know that even if you're only one person, with a very limited amount of time that there's something you can do in this area.

<u>Assessing your practice</u>

In assessing your practice you need to think of not only how many working lawyers there are but also how may assistants, secretaries and interns are working as well. If you're honest with your staff about what you're trying to do they may be willing to do some of the initial legwork for you in terms of getting contact names and finding out any specific requirements in addition to sending a press release or pitch.

You also need to be realistic about how much work everyone is doing already. If your practice is fairly new then there may be more downtime time which you'll need to decide how to direct. Ask yourself if it's more important to find additional clients or get some recognition in the news. There's no right or wrong answer to that question, you just have to be sure about the direction you want to go in.

Finally, you need to factor in how much time you'll need to put in personally. This is especially true if you're trying to secure radio interviews or television programs. While smaller stations or local shows may be willing to work around your schedule this won't be the case for the bigger outlets who develop their schedules months in advance. Also, be sure to think of a contingency plan in the event that a case comes up in the interim i.e. if you're able to book a television appearance in another state. Be sure to ask before you commit whether or not they have the capabilities to carry out a clear interview via phone or skype in the event that you can't physically be there to do work. There may be some shows that are unable to do this but its better that you know upfront so you don't make a commitment that you may have to break.

Best case scenario: You have the team and the time to put a great deal of effort into public relations and are at a point in your career when you feel its right for you to accept bookings beyond those that are local. In this case you'll want to proceed as follows:

    * Begin building a database of the news outlets where you'd like to see stories about your practice. This list should include magazines, newspapers, television shows and radio shows. Be sure to include the name of the outlet, the media contact person's title and the media contact person's name.[86]

    * Assign one person to be in charge of public relations. While other people in your office can and should contribute to the database you want any messages sent out to have a consistent tone and any replies to be sent to a single email address.

    * Begin to put together a database of who was contacted, when they were contacted and when a reply message was received. While this information may all be in an email account, you'll want an offline record of it as well.

Worst case scenario: You'll be flying solo with your public relations campaign and you don't have a lot of time to dedicate to it. In this case there's one really good thing that you can do:

---

86   Be sure to double check this information before sending anything out.

* Go to HARO[87] http://www.helpareporter.com/[88] and sign up as a source. Every day, Monday through Friday, you'll get three emails. Each of these emails will have information from reporters, websites radio shows and television shows all looking for stories. There may be days or even weeks when you don't find anything relevant. But when you do find something related to you or your practice all you have to do is send out a query letter by the requested deadline. This is a simple way for you to get some press even when you don't have a lot of free time to generate buzz on your own.

You know now:

* That you need to consider the size of your practice, the current workload and your schedule when assessing your practice.

* That you can move forward with a basic public relations plan even if you don't have a large staff or a lot of time.

You're now considering:

* The type of practice you have and the type of Public Relations you should move forward with.

Exercise: Select three media outlets that you'd like to see your practice mentioned in or that you'd like to be a guest on. Take some time to look for the specific contact information that you need to find. Is it easily accessible on their website or in their publication? Are there specific guidelines that you need to follow? How far in advance do they want you to submit a query? How long did it take you to find this information?

---

87   HARO stands for Help A Reporter Out.

88   More information on this site is available in the resources section.

Next: Traditional Marketing

Chapter 10: Traditional Marketing

Having spent the last three chapters addressing ways in which to get media to work for you and your marketing efforts, you may believe that there isn't anything else that you can or should be doing in that regard. That line of thinking is incorrect, though. There are a number of things you can do offline that will be just as, if not more effective, than digital marketing efforts. Utilizing one or more of these methods can greatly increase your ability to reach your market.

This chapter is separated into five parts.

The first part focuses on television. While marketing via a television campaign can be expensive it can also be highly efficient. When thinking about using television for your marketing efforts, it's necessary to consider the various avenues including commercials, appearances on talk shows and news programs and content created especially for public access.

By the end of part one you'll be able to do all of the following:

* Identify whether or not TV will be an appropriate marketing medium for you.

* Identify what type of TV spot you should work on if television is appropriate for you.

The second part focuses on radio. Similar to television spots, radio can be a costly route however there are numerous options, one of which may work for you and your practice.

By the end of part two you'll be able to do all of the following:

* Identify all of the ways in which you can utilize radio for your marketing.

* Identify what types of radio marketing will be most effective for your practice.

The third part focuses on print media. Marketing via this way can occur in numerous ways including traditional ads, advertorial content and interviews or other news pieces.

By the end of part three you'll be able to do all of the following:

* Identify the do's and don'ts of marketing via print media.

The fourth part focuses on direct mailers. These may be the most effective way for you to reach your market and should be considered a viable option.

By the end of part four you'll be able to do all of the following:

* Identify what types of direct mailers would be most effective for your market.

* Identify the best times to send direct mailers.

The fifth part focuses on sponsorships. Sponsorships can be a unique way to communicate with your market and should not be overlooked as they can be undertaken at various levels.

By the end of part five you'll be able to do all of the following:

* Identify the various do's and dont's of sponsorships.

What you'll need for this chapter:

* A pencil and a piece of paper or an empty computer file.

* An internet connection.

Television

96.7 percent of American households have a television and while that number is down from 98.9 percent[89] that's still a huge number of people who have access to television as a medium. Therefore, it's a good idea to consider whether or not marketing on television can be viable for your practice. It's also necessary to look at the numerous ways in which marketing on television can be done. While commercials are an option, they're not the only option and in that vein it's necessary to consider the power of both guest appearances and even creating your own content as alternatives.

Television commercials

When most people think about marketing on television their thoughts go to commercials. And there's a good reason for this. Commercials offer a message in a manner that's concise and often memorable, at times they can even create iconic characters which go on to define a brand. The thought of creating a commercial can be an alluring one but you have to be sure that you're considering all of the pros and cons. First, think about it this way: when is the last time you saw an ad for a lawyer on television? Now, think about that ad specifically. Chances are good that it fell into one of three categories: 1) It was for a major law firm, 2) It was on at around 3am or 3) It wasn't the greatest quality. The reason for this is simple: Television commercials are fairly expensive to produce. This is because no matter what you're paying for the commercial

89   http://www.forbes.com/sites/briancaulfield/2011/05/03/1-2-million-americans-households-just-killed-their-television/.

twice. First, you're paying to have the commercial produced; this includes a script, a crew and if necessary a location and actors. Fees for this can range but generally you're going to get what you pay for, so a crew you put together for next to nothing on Craigslist probably isn't going to create something of the same quality as the video production company that's been around for years. Second, you're paying to air the commercial and that fee can vary greatly and will depend on the station you're looking for the commercial to appear on and the hours you want it to run. Commercials on major networks during prime time hours are going to cost more than those on smaller networks during off hours. Depending on your practice, these costs may not be how you choose to spend your marketing budget as they could feasibly all go into this one effort.

Television appearances

In the last chapter we discussed the power of public relations. Now is a good time to utilize some of that knowledge, especially in terms of creating pitch letters. A well-crafted pitch letter, along with a timely press release, could help you to secure a slot on a talk show or a news program. It's worth noting that while the former may be a harder feat to achieve as such programs often have schedules which are pre-set months in advance that you should still look to see if the potential is there. In terms of news programs, consider that no matter where you're located your local news probably offers a "Contact Us" page. For example, NBC in New York has a contact page[90] which features a drop down menu asking specifically whether you're submitting a news tip or press release

---

90   http://www.nbcnewyork.com/contact-us/.

among other things. While such submissions are not a guarantee, they can offer you another potential television marketing opportunity.

Creating your own content

You may be thinking that creating your own content is going to be as (if not more) expensive than creating a commercial. It doesn't have to be though, especially if you utilize public access television. There are two ways in which this can be done, and both are fairly inexpensive.

* Utilize the public bulletin board. Most public access channels have a public bulletin board that airs on television. This is a way for information to be shared in a static manner as this isn't a commercial but literally a posting that shares information with the community. This is a good place to put information such as the fact that you're opening a new office or offering free consultations for a certain period. Every market varies in regards to the terms and conditions regarding how this bulletin board can be used, but in most markets it's free or low cost and posts run on a first come, first serve basis. The benefit for this is that no matter how new your practice, is this method is cost effective. However, you do have to be sure that you're aware of all deadlines associated with this service as well as any restrictions.

* Create your own show on public access. The costs associated with creating your own show on public access can be less expensive than you may initially be thinking. This is due to the fact that much of what airs on these channels isn't paid for based on viewers but rather by utilizing a different pay structure. You'll need to check with the station in your area but often times the cost is an annual or even one time fee. The benefit to this is that you can create content specifically targeted towards your

market. You will need to do market research though to ensure that your client base is watching public access television[91] and what type of content will appeal most to them.

You know now:

    * That over 90 percent of American households have televisions.

    * That there are numerous ways for you to market your legal practice on television.

    * That no matter what you'll end up paying for commercials twice, once to produce the content and again to air it.

    * That talk shows and news programs offer an additional way for you to market.

    * That it may be possible for you to contact your local news with a press release.

    * That public access channels offer two ways for you to air your own content.

    * That public bulletin boards offer free or low cost ways for you to make announcements on television.

    * That before investing in creating your own show on public access you need to do market research to determine whether your potential clients watch that type of programming and if the majority of them have access to it.

---

91   You also need to be aware of whether or not they even have these channels as some cable or satellite providers don't include these channels in their line-up.

You're now considering:

* What type of television marketing is best suited to your practice in terms of who your market is and the marketing budget that you have in place.

Exercise: Find your local public access station online. See if they have a public bulletin. If so, what are the restrictions that exist? Are the deadlines daily, weekly or monthly? Do you have anything that you could announce using this method?

Radio

Radio was one of the first forms of modern entertainment and its power shouldn't be discounted now. There are three key ways which you can utilize radio for your marketing efforts, the first is via radio advertising, the second is by appearing as a guest on radio programs and the third is producing your own radio show. All three options have pros and cons and should be explored fully before deciding which of these methods will work best for you.

Radio advertising

Similar to television commercials, radio ads are paid for twice, once to produce them and again to air them. However, the cost of advertising on radio is often a fraction of the cost of advertising on television. And when you factor in the prevalence of internet radio in addition to traditional radio stations, you have the power to reach a fairly wide audience, even when you're only broadcasting to a local audience. The primary benefit of a radio ad is the ability to re-air the ad on multiple stations and, depending on your market, smaller stations may suffice.

However, cost may still be a factor especially if your practice is new or has an extremely limited marketing budget in place.

Appearing as a guest on radio programs

Everything learned in the prior chapter about public relations can once again be utilized. By reaching out to radio show hosts it may be possible for you to market your practice on air without paying for airtime. Think about your market before you start writing your query letters. Consider whether a college station or independent station could serve your needs sufficiently. If so, I suggest contacting them first as they may have more flexibility in what they're able to air and less structured schedules which means that there could be less of a wait between the time you contact them and the time which you appear on air.

Producing your own content

Producing your own content can be easier than you think and the biggest factor may not be cost but rather time. If you do have the time though this could be a great way to target your potential clients specifically.

You know now:

* That there are three key ways to market your practice via radio.

* That radio advertisements, like television commercials are paid for twice since you have to pay to produce them and pay to air them.

* That college stations or independent stations may be good to contact about appearing on air based on your market.

* That producing your own content does not need to be expensive.

You're now considering:

    * What type of radio marketing is most effective for your law firm.

    * If you have the time to commit to producing your own content.

Try this: Go to http://www.gaebler.com/Radio-Ad-Rates.htm.[92] This site offers state-by-state radio advertising rates.

Try this: Go to http://www.blogtalkradio.com/.[93] This site will allow you to create your own internet based radio show starting at under $50/month.

Print media

    Even with e-books and tablets, there are still print newspapers and magazines in circulation. Depending on the market that you're trying to reach these may be the perfect format for getting information about your practice to them. There are some definite do's and don'ts that you need to keep in mind when using this medium though.

Do find more localized newspapers and magazines to contact if you're considering traditional ads. The rates will be lower and you'll have a better chance of reaching the exact audience that you're looking for.

Don't confuse quality with quantity. Yes, papers like the *Wall Street Journal* and the *New York Times* are highly respected but their quality is irrelevant if they won't reach your intended audience. This isn't to say that you shouldn't be concerned with the quality of the publication that you're marketing in but don't let that be the sole deciding factor.

---

92   More information on this site is available in the resources section.

Do think of methods other than advertisements when you're considering marketing in print. Consider utilizing your public relations knowledge to pitch stories to the local paper or think about putting together an advertorial.[94]

Don't discount free newspapers or magazines. Free newspapers and magazines are often niche related and may prove a bigger benefit to your marketing than you realize. For example, if you're an entertainment lawyer then a free publication for local musicians or the local art scene may be a good place to either place an ad or pitch a story.

Do look for specialized independent magazines that are print on demand or available in multiple formats. Print on demand magazines have created extreme niche markets and there may be a way for you to use this to your advantage by purchasing ad space or pitching content to one of these magazines. This could be especially viable if you're willing to travel.

You know now:

   * That local print magazines and newspapers offer your best bet for reasonable advertising rates.

   * That while quality is important, so is the amount of people in your market who'll be reached.

   * That there are methods other than direct ad placement for getting your marketing into print media.

---

93   More information on this site is available in the resources section.

94   "An advertisement promoting the interests or opinions of a corporate sponsor, often presented in such a way as to resemble an editorial." Definition from http://www.thefreedictionary.com/advertorial.

* That free newspapers and magazines may be a good place for your marketing efforts depending on what they specialize in.

* That specialized independent magazines may offer you another possibility for marketing.

You're now considering:

* If any of the newspapers or magazines local to your area would be a good fit for your marketing.

Try this: Go to http://www.magcloud.com/[95] and browse the available publications. Look at a category that's relevant to your practice. Are there any magazines that you think will appeal to your market? You may need to order a copy of the magazine in order to find out information on submissions and advertisements. But this could be a good way to find independent publications that could help expand your market.

Direct mailers

Direct mailers are one of the most effective ways to reach your market, primarily because they're targeted materials either sent out to a personal mailing list or as a part of a larger flier-based campaign. However, it's important to create direct mailers that stand out both from your competitors and from junk mail. You want to be sure that your mailing materials fit the following criteria so that they can make the maximum impact:

* Use quality paper stock. You don't want your mailers ruined because of rain, snow or even sun exposure. Additionally, if you use a heavier paper, a textured paper or something with a high gloss, there's a

---

95   More information on this site is available in the resources section.

133

greater likelihood that your mailer won't accidentally be tossed in the trash before it's looked at.

* Remember your market research. Consider the colors, images and types of information that will be most appealing to the people in your target market.

* Consider your copy carefully. Make sure that any text you put on your mailers isn't only easy to read but is also interesting to read. This is especially important when you're doing a mass mailing in an attempt to gain a larger market share. Include a random piece of trivia that's relevant to your practice, a shocking statistic or pose a question. You want to be sure that you're using something that's likely to instantly engage a reader.

* Include a call to action of some sort. Remember that not everyone who receives your mailer is going to need a lawyer and you don't want to be dismissed based solely on that fact. So be sure to provide whoever receives your mailer with a reason to visit your blog, website or Facebook page. This can be done simply by linking your call to action to your copy. For example, if you use your copy to pose a question then place the answer on one of your sites and let the reader know exactly where online they can find it.

* Don't forget to include contact information. While mailers will come from you and include the address to your practice, you also want to be sure to include a phone number and an email address. The more methods someone has to contact you, the more likely it is that they'll do so.

* Personalize mailers when possible. If you have a relatively small market, and incredibly neat handwriting then you may want to write the

message on the mailers by hand. People may be more responsive to such a gesture.

* Give people a way to opt out of future mailings. Not everyone you send out a mailer to is going to want to receive them in the future so give them the option to not receive mail from you in the future.

* Give people a way to sign up for additional information. You can use your mailers to get people to sign up for things such as your newsletters or podcasts. There may be people who don't immediately have a need for a lawyer who still want to be kept in the loop in the event that they do need one.

* Be courteous. Don't send multiple mailers in a single month in an attempt to test which of your marketing efforts may be most effective. You don't want to be seen as either desperate or a nuisance. The only exception to this is if there's a major error on your initial mailer like the wrong phone number.

* Do some research to see when your services are most likely to be needed. Check online to see when certain trends are on the rise in your part of the country. For example if you're an accident attorney you may want to look up the month that averages the highest amount of car crashes and concentrate your mailers to be sent out in that time period.

You know now:

* That direct mailers are an effective way to reach your target market.

* That you should use quality paper stock.

* That you need to keep your market research in mind.

* That your copy should be engaging.

* That you need to include a call to action.

* That contact information should be included.

* That you should personalize mailers when possible.

* That you should give people a way to opt out of future mailings.

* That you should give people a way to receive additional information.

* That multiple mailers shouldn't be sent out in a single month unless the second mailer is being sent to correct an error on the first.

* That research on trends relevant to your market can help you determine the best times to send out mailers.

You're now considering:

* What type of mailers would be most appealing to your market.

Exercise: Write out a fact or question that you think would engage your market. Is this information that's widely known? If so, how can you put your own spin on it? If not, do you think your market would care enough about it to follow the call to action on a mailer? How many of these facts and/or questions can you come up with over the course of a week?

Sponsorships

Sponsorships are one of the most innovative ways in which you can market your legal practice. You're not directly paying for advertisements and you're also taking the opportunity to support something that's important to you and those who you're marketing to. As with print media there are some fairly specific do's and don'ts that you should keep in mind when looking at sponsorship opportunities.

Do consider the financial commitment. Sponsorships can be fairly costly endeavors depending on what exactly it is you're sponsoring. Make sure you know exactly how much money it's going to cost you upfront, and if there are any additional costs you may be responsible for before committing to anything.

Don't sponsor something just because it'll get your name in front of a large group of people. While it is important that your name is seen you don't want to end up in a situation where your credibility is questioned because of what you choose to sponsor. For example, if you're an environmental attorney and a large percentage of your market is found to be vegan or vegetarian you don't want to alienate them by sponsoring a local pig roast.

Do consider if there's a time commitment. There are some sponsorship opportunities that will want you to be physically present for certain events. Ask if it would be possible to send a representative in your place if you're not able to attend.

Don't assume anything. Make sure that you get all of the sponsorship information in writing and that you ask about anything that's unclear. Also, if all of the paperwork isn't available at one time don't sign off on anything until it is.

Do personally promote your sponsorship efforts. Include information about it on your website, blog and social network pages.

Don't forget any important dates associated with your sponsorship. For example, if you're sponsoring a local little league team, make sure that you mark the dates of their games into your calendar and share that information as well.

Do consider memorializing projects as well. Think about donating a series of books to the library and having them include 'a donated by' card in the front[96] or buy a park bench and have the name of your practice placed on the plaque.[97]

You know now:

* That you need to consider the financial commitment of a sponsorship.

* That you shouldn't sponsor something if it may alienate your market.

* That you need to consider the time commitment.

* That you shouldn't assume anything about the sponsorship.

* That you should personally promote whatever it is you're sponsoring.

* That you should be aware of all dates associated with you're sponsorship.

* That you should think about memorializing opportunities.

---

96   You'll have to check with your local library to see if they do this.

You're now considering:

    * If there's anything or anyone in your local area currently looking for sponsorship that you can contribute to.

Try this: Go to http://www.adoptahighway.com/[98] and see if there's a sign in your local area that can be adopted.

Next: Values. Integrity. Persistence.

---

97   You'll have to check locally for these types of opportunities.

98   More information on this site is available in the resources section

Chapter 11: Values. Integrity. Persistence.

No matter which lawyer marketing strategies you choose to adopt, the size of your market or the size of your practice, there are three things that you always need to be focused on in order for you to be as successful as possible. There's no secret formula or magic beans, you just need to be sure that at all times you're acting ethically and that you're propelling yourself forward.

This chapter is separated into three parts.

The first part of this chapter focuses on values. It's necessary to realize that the word has a dual meaning and that both definitions apply to your legal marketing.

By the end of part one you'll be able to do all of the following:

* Identify which of your personal values are your most important asset.

* Identify the difference between true value and perceived value.

* Identify the importance of true value as it pertains to your practice.

* Identify the importance of perceived value as it pertains to your practice.

The second part of this chapter focuses on integrity. In terms of your practice, integrity is crucial and can be the difference between a short stint as a lawyer and long and fulfilling career in the legal profession.

By the end of part two you'll be able to do all of the following:

* Identify the importance of building a good reputation.

* Identify the importance of maintaining a good reputation.

* Identify the necessity of providing good customer service.

* Identify the benefits of cultivating and projecting a positive outlook.

The third part of this chapter focuses on persistence. You can be an amazing lawyer, but if you give up or decide not to work as hard after losing a case you may never reach your full potential.

By the end of part three you'll be able to do all of the following:

* Identify what you as a lawyer should have in common with a character from a children's book.

* Identify ways to motivate yourself to move forward.

* Identify how I personally ended up as the partner using persistence.

What you'll need for this chapter:

* A pencil and a piece of paper or an empty computer file.

* Your calendar or daily planner.[99]

* An internet connection.

Values

Values can be defined in two ways. One way values is defined is via the moral or ethical characteristics that a person deems as important. Another way value is defined is by describing the monetary amount that

---

99   It should include any events or activities that you have going on.

something is worth. Both definitions are necessary when considering legal marketing.

Personal values

Think fast:

What traits do you think are important?

Is there a motto or a creed that you live by?

Is that reflected in your practice?

These questions may not immediately seem as if they're relevant to marketing but I can assure that they are and if you look closely at almost any company in any industry you'll see that they operate in a way that at least takes these thoughts into mind. For example, in the healthcare sector, most hospitals make their mission, vision and value statements available to the public. The values are the traits which they find important. The vision is the motto or creed that they operate under. And the mission is the way in which that motto or creed is being reflected into their work. If your practice doesn't already operate this way, it's the way it needs to begin operating. Now. If you're at a loss trying to come up with something think of the questions in a different way:

What are the traits that you think are necessary to being successful? Are those traits things that you could feel good promoting?[100]

Are there any words, or a phrase that embody those traits? Can you take those traits and turn them into a personal mantra?

---

100   If it isn't something you'd tell your mother or teach to a small child it shouldn't be something you feel comfortable promoting, no matter how successful you think it might make you in the short-term.

How can those traits be reflected on a regular basis in the way that you work?

Take some time to seriously think about this. Consider who you are, what characteristics you think are crucial and the tangible ways in which those personality traits can be incorporated into your practice. These should be things that feel natural to you because they should be natural to you.

Monetary value

Monetary values can be looked at in one of two ways, either as true value or as perceived value. Both are important for your practice so it's important that you familiarize yourself.

True value

This is the actual monetary value that something has. Think about this the same way that you'd think about wholesale prices or the price it would actually cost to make something. It's the most honest assessment of price and yet it can also be incredibly tricky to justify when it's assigned to things such as time or expertise.

Perceived value

This is the monetary value that people assume something is worth and it can be dictated by any number of factors. For example, a product may be deemed of a higher quality because it has a recognized name on its label when in actuality it has the same basic ingredients and the same quantities as the generic brand.

True value vs Perceived value

Ultimately, in looking at true value versus perceived value what you're really looking at is actual quality versus what someone else is determining quality to be.

You may be wondering what this has to do with you and your practice. Well, it's important that you know that both true value and perceived value have a place in your practice.

Incorporating True value

True value needs to be incorporated into your practice in a number of crucial ways:

* Make sure that the client gets what they're paying for. This means working for them when you're supposed to be working for them. And only billing them for hours that you're actually handling their case.

* Make sure that you're more substance than show. An opulent office, expensive clothes and a new car are nice but they're not more important than your legal expertise.

* Make sure that you do your due diligence and do the necessary background research to ensure that any experts you employ work ethically.

Incorporating perceived value

Perceived value should not be dismissed. Before anyone is going to hire you they need to feel confident that you will not only do the job but that you'll do it well.

* Make sure that your appearance is always neat and clean. You don't need thousand dollar suits but anything you wear needs to fit well.

* Choose high quality business cards. Your cards don't need to be flashy per se but they should be on thick cardstock and well printed. It should also go without saying that the only company name on them should be yours so getting cards from a free service won't work.

* Proudly display your degrees and awards. These accolades act as a visual representation of your accomplishments and serve to reinforce them.

You know now:

* That both values as they pertain to the traits that you hold important, and value as it pertains to the monetary value of something are important to your practice.

* That your values need to be reflected in your practice.

* That true value refers to the actual value of something.

* That perceived value refers to what the believed value of something is.

* That both true value and perceived value have a place in your practice.

You're now considering:

* What your values are.

* Ways to incorporate true value into your practice.

* Ways to incorporate perceived value in your practice.

Exercise: Write out a mission, vision and values for your practice. Think of the questions asked earlier and craft something that honestly reflects you and what you hope to do with your career.

Integrity

There's an old joke that asks "How can you tell when a lawyer's lying?" The answer: "Their lips are moving." I kid you not, there are probably a million more just like that. I share that to say this; despite what we actually do, lawyers aren't looked at as having a great deal of integrity. The stereotype is an unfortunate one. And the fact that it's so widespread means that we have to work extra hard to combat it.

Building a good reputation

Reputation is perhaps more crucial in this business than it is in any other industry. As a lawyer you need to be sure that the reputation you're building up is one that you can be proud of. There are numerous ways that you can do this:

* Treat all of your clients with respect. Especially when they don't deserve it. Almost everyone has worked a job where there was at least one person who was incredibly difficult to deal with. And we all have a breaking point. Don't break in front of the client. Wait until they leave and then take five minutes for yourself. If you find that you really can't work with them then as politely as possible decline doing so.

* Don't overextend yourself. There are only 24 hours in a day and its not physically possible for you to work every one of them. It's better for you to have three clients who you do a stellar job for then to have ten clients who you only do an okay job for.

* Be honest about your skills. It may be tempting to exaggerate about what you can do but if you're hired based on those padded qualifications and can't deliver you'll end up looking bad.

* Make sure that any interest you express is genuine. During small talk with clients don't act overly enthusiastic about something that in truth you couldn't care less about. While it may be necessary for you to listen to a story or two about something you don't really care about it, don't gush over it as it could backfire in the future.

* Fight fairly. Whenever you're in court there's nothing wrong with using all of the legal resources that you have at your disposal. Just make sure that everything you're doing falls clearly within the bounds of the law.

Maintaining a good reputation

The only thing more difficult than building a good reputation is working to maintain that reputation throughout your career. However there are some ways in which that process can be made easier.

* Be consistent. Treat all of your clients and all of your cases similarly. Of course there will be cases that require more attention or clients that you have a greater affinity for. But you shouldn't operate with blatant favoritism.

* Be charitable. Giving of yourself in some way is a great way for you to maintain a good reputation. Choose a charity that is truly important to you so that you can sing its praises honestly and remember that you don't need to pledge money, you can also volunteer.

Additionally, you'll want to provide good customer service and keep a positive outlook. Both of these factors should be looked at more in depth.

Providing good customer service

Providing good customer service is about more than making sure that the coffee is always fresh or that your receptionist has good phone etiquette. Those things are certainly important but there are things that are even more critical.

* Admit when you make a mistake. If you notice an error in a client's bill, accidentally file the wrong motion or do anything else that can threaten your credibility if exposed you have to own up to it. Don't get in the habit of covering up little mistakes because it will only lead to covering up big mistakes. Fess up, fix it and move forward.

* Don't become overly involved in the life of a client. In representing someone you learn a lot about them, some of which is crucial to your case and some of which is minutia that you really don't need to know. While this advice may seem to fly in the face of providing the best possible customer service it's important that the relationships that you have with clients remain professional. Otherwise your judgment may become clouded.

* Make sure that you meet or exceed expectations. Whether you realize it or not you control what the majority of what people expect from you based on what you present in your marketing materials and how you treat other clients. With that in mind keep your marketing message realistic and always be aware of how you're treating people.

Cultivating and keeping a positive outlook

In order to cultivate and keep a positive outlook you need to ensure that you're doing two things. You need to be aware of what's being projected around you and the manner in which you deal with your competition.

Projection

Positive projections aren't necessarily self-promotion. And it isn't about tooting your own horn. Or rather it isn't only about tooting your own horn. A person who constantly brags about their achievements or talks about nothing but their own success is generally viewed as either boring or with the thought that they're overcompensating for something. There are a number of nonverbal ways to promote a positive outlook for both yourself and your practice.

* Dress for success. I know that I've already mentioned the importance of a certain appearance in terms of perceived value. And I'm mentioning it again here because how you look really is relevant. We've all heard the saying that you shouldn't judge a book by its cover but the truth is that books with appealing covers are probably more likely to be selected. And if you don't look like you believe in what you do, you can't really expect anyone else to believe it either.

* Keep focal points in your office. Consider why it is you became a lawyer and what it is that gets you out of bed and into the office every morning. Maybe you work so hard because of your family or maybe you're saving up for a Ferrari. Whatever the reason, keep a reminder of it

somewhere in your office.[101] This reminder will help you get through the tougher days.

　　* Declare your office a drama-free zone. When you're working long hours with the same group of people their negative qualities can become amplified at an accelerated pace. There's no foolproof way to keep everyone you employ happy with each other but you need to keep your eyes open and recognize when trouble may be brewing. You don't want your employees to be sidetracked by petty dramas when they're supposed to be working.

Dealing with the competition

　　If you're really the better lawyer you don't need to bad-mouth your competition in order to prove it. It's that simple. You gain nothing by hurling insults or insinuating improprieties. Think about it this way would you rather stay at a hotel that advertised all of its positive qualities or one which focused instead on everything that was wrong with the other hotels in the area? When you get caught up with what makes something inferior you often forget to promote your own positive attributes.

You know now:

　　* That as a lawyer you need to work especially hard to prove that you have integrity.

　　* That there are numerous ways to build a good reputation.

　　* That maintaining a good reputation is harder than developing one in the first place.

101　　If you're uncomfortable having pictures of loved ones in your office, think of another way to represent them like with one of their favorite books on your bookshelf.

* That customer service extends into all areas of your practice.

* That there are two ways to cultivate and keep a positive outlook.

* That talking badly about your competition doesn't do you any good.

You're now considering:

* Ways that you can personally boost your reputation.

* Ways that you can keep your work place harmonious.

Try this: If you have a more relaxed office atmosphere check out http://turntable.fm/[102] as a good way to help foster office unity may be through sharing your music.

Persistence

Persistence is the key to success and propelling yourself forward the right way is what you should always be doing.

The lesson you can learn from a children's book

It's almost certain that you've heard the phrase "I think I can, I think I can..." That phrase comes from a very popular children's book *The Little Engine That Could.* Do you think you can? If not, then rest assured after a while no one else will either.

Motivate yourself

You may not always feel like pushing yourself forward or going that extra step. There are days that are harder than others and you may

---

102   More information on this site is available in the resources section.

even have moments where you want to give up and do something else. But provided those are just passing moments and for the most part you love what you do, you need to find ways to work past that.

* Realize that you're not a superhero. And that no one really expects you to be. By taking this extra pressure off of yourself it may be easier to do your job and do it to the best of your abilities.

* Set goals for yourself. By creating a list of short term and long term goals you give yourself things to work towards and look forward to.

* Reward yourself for your accomplishments. Treat yourself after a difficult win or after you've reached a milestone. This may give you enough incentive to keep achieving those types of things.

* Remind yourself why you became a lawyer in the first place. Sometimes thinking about that initial motivating force can help move you forward.

How I became partner: My own tale of persistence

I grew up very close to my uncle. He was a personal injury attorney, one of the first to advertise on television and incredibly successful because of his marketing. Because of this I always knew I wanted to be a lawyer and for a long time I thought I would follow his footsteps. But in 2003 I met the man who served as my mentor. He was an asset protection lawyer and I was instantly drawn to what he did for a living. I found it fascinating and began reading books on the subject including those by my mentor. However, when I graduated law school I didn't immediately go into asset protection. I wanted the experience of trying cases so instead I became a prosecutor. Shortly afterwards I opened my own asset protection firm. But being new I would also take other cases as well.

During this time I called my mentor again. He'd worked with my friends and family securing their assets and probably assumed that I was looking for something similar. I wasn't. I was looking for a job. I researched everything I could about the company and even memorized minute details like the color of the tie he was wearing in photos on his website. I met with him and presented myself as someone ready to work. There weren't any openings though. Rather than back down. I told him that I'd work for free for three months and that if during that time I didn't prove to be the best employee ever I'd go away. I left that meeting feeling great; I sent a thank you card the next day and followed up in a few weeks only to be told that I couldn't be hired, even for free.

There are plenty of people who would have given up at this point. Not me. I responded by hiring him to handle my asset protection. Luckily for me his fees were really reasonable and there were no upfront costs. I asked him every question I could think of and took the time we had together to build a relationship. I also showed him that I was capable of bringing in clients by referring pro athletes to him. I wasn't technically working for him but I was working for him. I spent months building this relationship and when it came up in conversation that we'd be attending the same seminar I made sure that we were on the same flight, staying at the same hotel and sitting next to each other. We had lunch and dinner together, and we became friends.

In fact, we were so friendly at this point that when we returned home, we actually started working on a project together, an organization for asset protection lawyers where they could all learn from each other. It had been a year a half since I originally met him and I was still hopeful that I would get a chance to work for him eventually. But even I didn't expect what happened next.

I got a call one day to come into his office, this was a rarity since while we did see each other regularly it wasn't more than once or twice a month and I'd already seen him that past weekend. He told me that there were times in our lives when we were meant to go up and that this was one of those times for me. He handed me the keys to his office. This was a man who at one point wouldn't hire me for free and now was making me a 50/50 partner in his firm.

You know now:

* That most of what you needed to learn about persistence your probably heard in kindergarten.

* That there are numerous ways to motivate yourself.

* That being persistent works not only in theory but also in practice which is where it counts.

You're now considering:

* If there's anything in particular that motivates you and helps you to move forward.

Exercise: Write out a way in which being persistent has gotten you something you wanted. It doesn't need to be related to the law. And it doesn't need to be long. This will however serve as a reminder of how you've utilized persistence.

Next: Resources

Resources

Chapter 1: Marketing Basics

https://www.toggl.com/. Toggl is a website that helps you track the time you spend doing each project. It can be a good way to help determine what aspects of your practice are currently taking what percentage of your time. Additionally, it can also be used across a variety of platforms making it easy to implement and use. Both free and paid plans are available.

http://office.microsoft.com/en-us/templates/marketing-budget-plan-TC001145556.aspx. Here you'll find a free template to help you with your marketing budget.

Chapter 2: Knowing Your Market

http://www.footprintlive.com/. This website acts as an add-on to Google Analytics and can track things such as visitor paths. This will give you better insight into your market from a digital perspective as it'll show you the search terms being used as well as where visitors to your website are coming from. While your visitors remain anonymous this site will help you gather general information such as location, which can help identify where your customer base may be concentrated.

Chapter 3: Carving Your Niche

http://www.humanmetrics.com/cgi-win/jtypes2.asp. This website will provide you with an online personality test. It can be a great way to assess what type of person you are in an unbiased and objective way.

http://www.businessdictionary.com is a comprehensive online list of business and marketing terms and definitions.

Chapter 4: Branding

https://bubbl.us/. This website will allow you to brainstorm online. It may be more effective than a sheet of paper and a pencil and will allow you to visually map out the commonalities between your clients.

http://www.plastekcards.com/. This website features plastic business cards. Such cards are a durable and memorable alternative to more standard paper cards. There are both customizable and pre-designed cards to create or choose from.

https://www.elance.com. This is a free website that allows you to post jobs or browse professionals by skill set.

http://www.craigslist.com. This is the main page for Craigslist and will lead you to any of the branches of the site based on state first.

http://fiverr.com/. This website specializes in getting projects done for the fee of $5. The graphics and advertising sections are good places to start.

Chapter 5: Becoming an Expert

http://750words.com/. This is an online only resource that provides writers at all levels to take part in a private writing exercise where the only goal is to write 750 words. This may be a good way to begin if you find yourself at a loss regarding what to write.

http://www.ezinearticles.com/. Once you have written your first article this website will allow you to upload it.

http://www.BrooklinePress.com. is a publishing house that caters to authors at all levels.

http://www.99designs.com/ is a website where you can launch contest to help you design covers for books, websites, banner ads, brochure designs and more.

http://moodle.com/. This is a site where you can set up online courses. These courses can be offered on a variety of subjects and you have control over who can see your content and when.

http://www.fullcalendar.com. While this site is only available in certain areas, it will help to promote your event or speaking engagement to a variety of different outlets. It is fee based so plan accordingly.

Http://www.thepodcasthost.com. This is a free podcasting website that will allow you to create, manage and even list your podcast on iTunes. Additional features include the ability to host a blog on the same site along with customizable themes and tutorials.

http://www.tungle.me/Home/. This website will help you keep your speaking engagements straight once you begin to book them.

http://www.khanacademy.org/about. A free math academy. Look at this site as an example of the way in which valuable content can be offered.

http://www.pixton.com. This is a site that allows you to create online comics. Use it to get your creativity flowing or if you think it'll appeal to your audience create a comic specifically for them. Use the free version to get the hang of creating them and then switch to a business account. The business account is a pay-as-you-go model which offers enhanced and exclusive features as well as the ability to utilize the content on social networks.

http://www.roku.com/developer. This site offers information on creating a channel specifically for the Roku. While you will need to learn their development language or hire someone who already knows it, it's a good way to get your content to subscribers who are looking for exactly what you're offering.

http://audacity.sourceforge.net/. Audacity is free, open source, cross-platform software for recording and editing sounds. Audacity is available for Windows®, Mac®, GNU/Linux® and other operating systems.

Chapter 6: Networking

http://www.linkedin.com/. This website is home to the largest professional network on the internet and boasts over 150 million members and is available in sixteen languages. Additionally, it offers numerous productivity tools for connecting with other members including the Outlook social connector which seamlessly integrates with Microsoft Outlook and allows users to do things like access connections directly from their inbox.

http://www.branchout.com. This is the largest professional networking service on Facebook. It allows users to find jobs, get leads, seek out talent and build better working relationships. Currently it is only available to Facebook users.

http://www.meetup.com. This site allows users to meet online in order to plan offline events in their local areas. You can either join an existing meet-up group or begin one of your own.

http://www.hallmark.com/online/. This site will allow you to add and update an address book to make e-card sending easier for important dates.

https://www.referralkey.com/. This website helps you build and maintain a network of reciprocal referrals. The site works in three key ways allowing you to 1) receive referrals from colleagues 2) promote your business every time you post and 3) get free leads from consumers in your area.

http://www.aceofsales.com/. Ace of Sales is an online newsletter company that allows you to send personalized newsletters to all of your email recipients. On top of newsletters, Ace of Sales allows you to send personalized greeting cards to recipients.

Chapter 7: Making Media Work: Social Media

https://lujure.com. This is a site that will allow you to build a customized front page for your professional profile. There are drag and drop options which make it easy to use and plans range from free to $300 per month. The best features may be the fact that you don't need to know any coding and that the set-up is meant to be incredibly quick.

http://trendsmap.com/. This site features real-time mapping of Twitter trends as they're occurring across the world. Since the trend topics are superimposed over a map you can focus on the region you're interested in specifically. One of the best features is that you can click on any one of the words or phrases being trended and see the tweets being posted to see if they'll be relevant for you.

http://timely.is/#/. You provide this site with your Twitter ID and it analyzes your last 199 tweets to see if they reached their maximum impact. If your tweets aren't having as much impact as they could be the service will tweet for you. All you have to do is add your tweets in advance and the site will post them when they'll have the most impact. This is a free service that is definitely worth a try.

http://twtvite.com/. This is a site which allows you to schedule a tweet-up so that you can meet your followers in person.

www.slideroll.com. This is a free service which allows users to create slide shows that can then be uploaded to YouTube. Additionally the slide shows can also be added to social media sites such as Facebook or sent to recipients directly via email.

http://pinterest.com/ is a visual bookmarking site which allows users to pin their online finds to virtual boards.

http://facebook.com/ is a social utility website that connects people with friends and others who work, study and live around them.

http://twitter.com/. Twitter is a real-time information network that uses 'tweets' to disseminate concise information to the public. You can use hashtags to group your posts as searchable.

http://www.youtube.com/ is a video sharing website where people can watch and share videos that they created.

Chapter 8: Making Media Work: Online Marketing

http://www.google.com/analytics/. This site offers free website analytics which allows for the user to track e-commerce campaigns and track specific goals. Additionally you can customize the site in order to ensure that you're getting the exact data you want and need.

http://cloudflood.com/. This site drives organic traffic to your website via the Facebook posts and Tweets of your clients which they post in exchange for free content. This content can be in the form of informational PDFs and similar digital content.

http://www.scorpiondesign.com/. This is a web design firm that focuses on lawyer websites. Their own website serves as a prime example of many of the components that they can add into a site in order to make it both dynamic and unique. Additionally, they offer complete customization and offer constant and consistent support.

http://blogcarnival.com/bc/index.php is a site that hosts blog carnivals. The benefit of writing for a blog carnival is that each one is a collection of blogs on a similar topic so readers looking through one are more likely to be interested in what you have to write about.

http://www.freeconferencecall.com/. This site only requires that the user provide their name and a valid email address in order to access the service. While domestic long distance charges are charged by your phone provider you can use this service for a teleconference with up to 96 different participants. Additionally, this service can be used to record interviews which you can use on your site.

http://simplebooklet.com/. This site allows users to create full color booklets which can be posted online. Unlike traditional newsletters which have limited functionality, this site allows for the addition of not just text and images but also videos and music. Additionally, it has built in sharing tools which allow for others to post it on the web as well.

adwords.google.com/. This site allows you to create ads that will appear on Google. It allows you to search for keywords ideas to best optimize your ads. Plus the cost structure is user friendly allowing you to set your budget with no minimum requirement and only paying when ads are clicked as opposed to paying just because they're displayed.

Chapter 9: Making Media Work: Public Relations

http://emsincorporated.com/ is a public relations company that you could use to obtain requests for radio, print placement and TV interviews.

http://www.prweb.com. This site offers additional insight on how to write a press release. More importantly however it distributes your press release to major search engines and to bloggers once it's uploaded and provides analytics for you to track the impact that your release is having.

http://www.marketwire.com. This is another website for press releases that you could use.

http://www.helpareporter.com/. This site allows you to become a source for a variety of reporters. Sign up for free, select your areas of expertise and during the week HARO will send you emails containing what reporters are looking for. If you see a story that you can help with, simply respond to the email address provided before the deadline and if the reporter believes you can be of assistance he'll contact you.

Chapter 10: Traditional Marketing

http://www.gaebler.com/Radio-Ad-Rates.htm. This site offers state-by-state radio advertising rates. It's a good place to start to see whether or not you can afford advertising rates on the stations that are most frequently listened to by your market.

http://www.blogtalkradio.com. This site will allow you to create your own internet based radio show. It offers a variety of services at both free and three premium levels which allow you to work within your budget.

The site features demos and tutorials via their BlogTalk university section. Additionally, as a business you can contact them regarding setting up a branded channel.

http://www.magcloud.com/. This is a site offering both print and digital magazines, many of which are independently published and produced. It features an online storefront and print copies will ship worldwide.

http://www.adoptahighway.com/. This site provides information on how you can adopt a stretch of highway. You need to contact the company directly regarding pricing and areas which are available however all signs purchased will feature your company name and full color logo.

Chapter 11: Becoming a V.I.P.

http://turntable.fm/. This site connects people by sharing their music with each other in real time. It may be a good way to connect in a more informal office setting.

Thank you!

Thank you for choosing this book to help you enhance your knowledge about Lawyer Marketing. Please feel free to reach out to me personally if you have any additional questions or are looking for a more personalized consultation.

Questions? Want to contact the author about one of the following:

1. With comments about this book.

2. For an online Lawyer Marketing newsletter.

3. For Mr. Presser to speak at a seminar or meeting.

4. For a complimentary **confidential**, preliminary marketing consultation.

Call Today 954-354-1990

www.LawyerMarketingLLC.com

Info@LawyerMarketingLLC.com

To order additional Brookline Press books visit

www.BrooklinePress.com or call 561-953-1322